Rick Steves

POCKET

MUNICH
& SALZBURG

Rick Steves with Gene Openshaw

Contents

Introduction

Munich ("München" in German), often called Germany's most livable city, is also one of its most historic, artistic, and entertaining. It's big and growing, with a population of 1.5 million. Until 1871, it was the capital of an independent Bavaria. Its royal palaces, jewels, and grand boulevards remind visitors that Munich has long been a political and cultural powerhouse. Meanwhile, the concentration camp memorial in nearby Dachau reminds us that a century ago, Munich provided a springboard for Nazism.

Get oriented in Munich's old center, with its colorful pedestrian zones. Immerse yourself in the city's art and history—crown jewels, Baroque theater, Wittelsbach palaces, great paintings, and beautiful parks. Spend your Munich evenings in a frothy beer hall or outdoor *Biergarten* amidst an oompah, bunny-hopping, and belching Bavarian atmosphere.

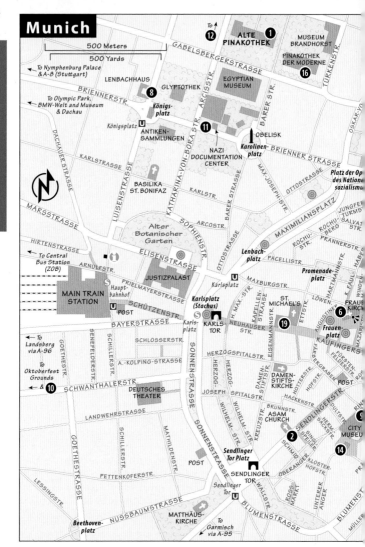

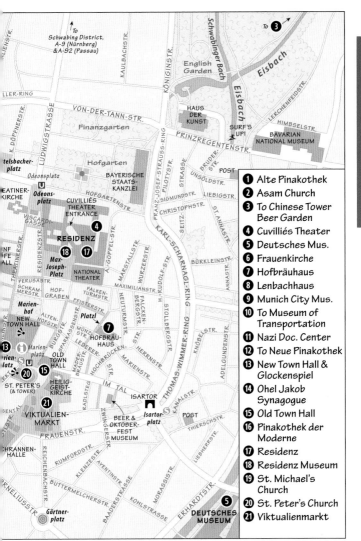

1 Alte Pinakothek
2 Asam Church
3 To Chinese Tower Beer Garden
4 Cuvilliés Theater
5 Deutsches Mus.
6 Frauenkirche
7 Hofbräuhaus
8 Lenbachhaus
9 Munich City Mus.
10 To Museum of Transportation
11 Nazi Doc. Center
12 To Neue Pinakothek
13 New Town Hall & Glockenspiel
14 Ohel Jakob Synagogue
15 Old Town Hall
16 Pinakothek der Moderne
17 Residenz
18 Residenz Museum
19 St. Michael's Church
20 St. Peter's Church
21 Viktualienmarkt

About This Book

Rick Steves Pocket Munich is a personal tour guide...in your pocket. The core of the book is seven chapters featuring self-guided walks and tours that zero in on Munich and the surrounding region's greatest sights and experiences.

My Munich City Walk starts at ground zero, Marienplatz, and guides you through the heart of the city, giving you a great orientation for your future sightseeing. At the Residenz, you can ogle the opulent rooms and priceless bling of the city's ruling family, the Wittelsbachs; at Nymphenburg you'll see their gardens, summer palace, and royal stables. The Museum Quarter museums take you through art history, from the Renaissance to Warhol, with a self-guided tour of the Alte Pinakothek—including Dürer's intense self-portrait. One of the most sobering and thought-provoking experiences in all of Europe is a visit to the Dachau Concentration Camp Memorial. In Bavaria, you can tour the fairy-tale Neuschwanstein Castle built by "Mad" (or merely inspired) King Ludwig II. And a day trip (or overnight stay) at Salzburg opens up a whole new world of Mozart, Alpine scenery, and *The Sound of Music*.

The rest of this book is a traveler's tool kit, with my best advice on how to save money, plan your time, use public transportation, and avoid lines at the busiest sights. You'll also get recommendations on hotels, restaurants, and activities.

Munich by Neighborhood

Despite its large population, Munich feels small—without skyscrapers and with streets that are friendly to pedestrians and bikers.

The tourist's Munich is circled by a ring road (the former path of the Old Town wall), with the bull's-eye being the city center—Marienplatz. Most of the sights and hotels I recommend are within a 20-minute walk of Marienplatz and each other. The excellent public transportation system makes even sights outside the inner ring accessible.

Think of Munich as a series of neighborhoods, cradling major landmarks.

Old Town—Inside the Ring: Marienplatz, in the middle of the ring, is a lively pedestrian zone of sights, shopping, and restaurants. Slicing west-to-east through the ring is a mostly pedestrianized street that changes names as it runs from the train station through

Munich's Neighborhoods

To Olympic Park, BMW-Welt and Museum & Dachau

NEUE PINAKOTHEK

ALTE PINAKOTHEK

PINAKOTHEK DER MODERNE

MUSEUM QUARTER

LENBACH-HAUS

Königsplatz

To Nymphenburg

NAZI DOCUMENTATION CENTER

OBELISK

ENGLISH GARDEN

HOF-GARTEN

SURF'S UP!

Odeonsplatz

RESIDENZ

TRAIN STATION

Karlsplatz

FRAUEN-KIRCHE

NEW TOWN HALL

Haupt-bahnhof

Karlsplatz

KAUFINGERSTR.

HOFBRÄU-HAUS

OLD TOWN

Marienplatz

To Oktoberfest Grounds

Sendlinger Tor

VIKTUALIEN-MARKT

Isartor

Isar River

Not to Scale

DEUTSCHES MUSEUM

Marienplatz to the Isartor gate (a 20-minute walk). The main S-Bahn line runs underground along this same east-west corridor. Around the ring, three gates survive from the city walls: Karlstor (west), Isartor (east), and Sendlinger Tor (south). North of Marienplatz, your landmark is the Residenz palace. South of Marienplatz are the Viktualienmarkt open-air market and some recommended hotels.

Train Station: A five-minute walk west of the ring is the main train station (Hauptbahnhof), home to many services (lockers, bike rental). Many recommended hotels and restaurants are nearby.

Museum Quarter: Several art museums (and other sights) cluster together in this neighborhood of broad leafy boulevards (north of the train station, near the Königsplatz U-Bahn stop).

English Garden: To the northeast of the ring stretches this vast

Munich and Nearby at a Glance

INTRODUCTION

In Munich's Center

▲▲ **Marienplatz** Munich's main square, at the heart of a lively pedestrian zone, watched over by New Town Hall and its glockenspiel. **Hours:** Glockenspiel jousts daily at 11:00 and 12:00, plus 17:00 March-Oct; New Town Hall tower elevator runs daily 10:00-19:00; Oct-April Mon-Fri 10:00-17:00, closed Sat-Sun. See page 16.

▲▲**Viktualienmarkt** Munich's "small-town" open-air market, great for a quick snack or meal. **Hours:** Market closed Sun; beer garden open daily 10:00-22:00 (weather permitting). See page 23.

▲▲**Hofbräuhaus** World-famous beer hall, worth a visit even if you're not chugging. **Hours:** Daily 9:00-late. See page 36.

▲▲**The Residenz** Elegant family palace of the Wittelsbachs, awash in Bavarian opulence. Complex includes the Residenz Museum (lavish apartments), Residenz Treasury (Wittelsbach family crowns and royal knickknacks), and the impressive, heavily restored Cuvilliés Theater. **Hours:** Museum and treasury—daily 9:00-18:00, mid-Oct-mid-March 10:00-17:00; theater—generally Mon-Sat 14:00-18:00, Sun from 9:00, longer hours Aug-mid-Sept. See page 43.

▲▲**Alte Pinakothek** Bavaria's best painting gallery, with wonderful European masters from the 14th through 19th century. **Hours:** Tue 10:00-20:30, Wed-Sun until 18:00, closed Mon. See page 55.

▲▲**Lenbachhaus** Three stages of German art: 19th-century, Blue Rider, and post-WWI. **Hours:** Tue-Sun 10:00-18:00, Thu until 20:00, closed Mon. See page 61.

▲▲**Nazi Documentation Center** Thoughtful look at Munich's role in the rise of Nazism. **Hours:** Tue-Sun 10:00-19:00, closed Mon. See page 86.

▲**Egyptian Museum** Easy-to-enjoy collection of ancient treasures. **Hours:** Tue 10:00-20:00, Wed-Sun until 18:00, closed Mon. See page 63.

▲**Munich City Museum** The city's history in five floors. **Hours:** Tue-Sun 10:00-18:00, closed Mon. See page 84.

▲**Asam Church** Private church of the Asam brothers, dripping with Baroque. **Hours:** Sat-Thu 9:00-19:00, Fri from 13:00. See page 28.

▲**Pinakothek der Moderne** Munich's modern art museum with works by Picasso, Dalí, Miró, Magritte, and Ernst. **Hours:** Tue-Sun 10:00-18:00, Thu until 20:00, closed Mon. See page 61.

▲**English Garden** The largest city park on the Continent, packed with locals, tourists, surfers, and nude sunbathers. (On a bike, I'd rate this ▲▲.) See page 87.

▲**Deutsches Museum** Germany's version of our Smithsonian Institution, with 10 miles of science and technology exhibits at its main branch. **Hours:** Daily 9:00-17:00. See page 87.

Outside Munich's City Center
▲▲▲**Dachau Concentration Camp Memorial** Notorious Nazi camp, now a powerful museum and memorial. **Hours:** Daily 9:00-17:00. See page 73.

▲▲**Nymphenburg Palace** The Wittelsbachs' impressive summer palace and vast park. **Hours:** Park—daily 6:00-dusk; palace buildings—daily 9:00-18:00, mid-Oct-March 10:00-16:00. See page 65.

▲**BMW-Welt and Museum** Futuristic museum and floating-cloud showroom, highlighting BMW past, present, and future in unforgettable architecture. **Hours:** BMW-Welt showroom exhibits—daily 9:00-20:00; museum—Tue-Sun 10:00-18:00, closed Mon. See page 89.

Day Trips
▲▲▲**Neuschwanstein Castle** Europe's most-photographed castle, nestled in a Bavarian wonderland. **Hours:** Tickets sold daily 7:30-17:00, mid-Oct-March 8:30-15:30. See page 126.

▲▲▲**Hohenschwangau Castle** King Ludwig's boyhood home, a less famous but more historic castle than nearby Neuschwanstein. **Hours:** Same hours as Neuschwanstein. See page 131.

▲▲▲**Salzburg** Elegant Austrian town with a castle, cathedral, shops, restaurants, scenery, and classical music almost nightly. **Hours:** Other than the ▲▲**Salzburg Museum** (closed Mon) and ▲▲**DomQuartier Museums** (closed Tue), most sights are open daily. See page 139.

▲**Andechs Monastery** Baroque church, hearty food, and Bavaria's best brew, in the nearby countryside. **Hours:** Beer garden Mon-Fri 11:00-20:00, Sat-Sun from 10:00, church open until 18:00. See page 92.

expanse of parkland and trails dotted with beer gardens and naked sunbathers.

Away from the Center: Within a short ride on public transit are many major sights, such as the BMW complex and Dachau Concentration Camp Memorial (north) and Nymphenburg Palace (northwest). The Oktoberfest grounds are a 15-minute walk southwest of the train station.

Day Trips: This book features two destinations—Neuschwanstein Castle and the Austrian city of Salzburg—that are each doable as a day trip (or overnight stay) from Munich.

Planning Your Time

The following day plans give an idea of how much an organized, motivated, and caffeinated person can see. Munich is worth two days, including a half-day spent at the Dachau Concentration Camp Memorial (45 minutes from the center by public transportation).

Day 1: If all you have is one day, follow my "Munich City Walk" (visiting museums along the way), tour one of the royal palaces (the Residenz or Nymphenburg), and drink in the beer-hall culture for your evening's entertainment (at the Hofbräuhaus or a less-obvious choice).

Day 2: With a second day, choose from the following: Tour the Dachau memorial, rent a bike to enjoy the English Garden, or—if you're into art—visit the Alte Pinakothek.

Day 3: With a third day, pick among Munich's many other worthwhile sights, such as the BMW-Welt and Museum, Deutsches Museum, or more of the Museum Quarter. You'll find plenty of suggestions in the More Munich Sights chapter.

With More Time: It's an all-day time commitment to visit either Salzburg or Neuschwanstein, but well worth it.

When to Go

Peak season (roughly May-Sept) offers the best weather, long days (light until after 21:00), and the busiest schedule of tourist fun. Late spring and fall generally have decent weather and lighter crowds. Winter can be cold and dreary, but Germany's famous Christmas markets brighten main squares from late November until Christmas.

Rick's Free Audio Tours and Video Clips

Rick Steves Audio Europe, a free app, makes it easy to download my audio tours and listen to them offline as you travel. For this book (look for the 🎧), free audio tours cover my Munich City Walk and Salzburg Town Walk. The app also offers my public radio show interviews with travel experts from around the globe. Scan the QR code on the inside front cover to find it in your app store, or visit RickSteves.com/AudioEurope.

Rick Steves Classroom Europe, a powerful tool for teachers, is also useful for travelers. This video library contains about 600 short clips excerpted from my public television series. Enjoy these videos as you sort through options for your trip and to better understand what you'll see in Europe. Check it out at Classroom.RickSteves.com.

Before You Go

You'll have a smoother trip if you tackle a few things ahead of time. For more details on these topics, see the Practicalities chapter and RickSteves.com, which has helpful travel-tip articles and videos.

Make sure your travel documents are valid. If your passport is due to expire within six months of your ticketed date of return, you need to renew it. Allow 12 weeks or more to renew or get a passport. Be aware of any entry requirements, and pack a copy of your vaccine record (or store it on your phone). Get passport and country-specific travel info at Travel.State.gov.

Arrange your transportation. Book your international flights. Figure out your transportation options. It's worth thinking about buying train tickets online in advance, as well as getting a rail pass, renting a car, or booking cheap European flights. (You can wing it once you're there, but it may cost more.)

Book rooms well in advance, especially if your trip falls during peak season or any major holidays or festivals.

Reserve ahead for key sights. Make reservations or buy tickets in advance for major sights, such as Neuschwanstein Castle. For

a BMW factory tour, sign up well in advance. Tickets for the music-packed Salzburg Festival (mid-July through August) go fast; buy tickets as early as possible (on sale online in January).

Consider travel insurance. Compare the cost of insurance to the cost of your potential loss. Understand what protections your credit card might offer and whether your existing insurance (health, homeowners, or renters) covers you and your possessions overseas.

Manage your money. "Tap-to-pay" or "contactless" cards are widely accepted and simple to use. You may need your credit card's PIN for some purchases—request it if you don't have one. Alert your bank that you'll be using your debit and credit cards in Europe. You don't need to bring euros; you can withdraw euros from ATMs in Europe.

Use your smartphone smartly. Sign up for an international service plan to reduce your costs, or rely on Wi-Fi in Europe instead. Download any apps you'll want on the road, such as maps, translators, and Rick Steves Audio Europe (see sidebar).

Pack light. You'll walk with your luggage more than you think. I travel for weeks with a single carry-on bag and a day pack. Use the packing checklist in Practicalities as a guide.

Travel Smart

If you have a positive attitude, equip yourself with good information (this book), and expect to travel smart, you will.

Pickpockets abound in crowded places where tourists congregate. Treat commotions as smokescreens for theft. Keep your passport and backup cash and cards secure in a money belt tucked under your clothes; carry only a day's spending money and a card in your front pocket or wallet.

If you wilt easily, choose a hotel with air-conditioning, start your day early, take a midday siesta, and resume your sightseeing later.

Be sure to schedule in slack time for picnics, laundry, people-watching, leisurely dinners, shopping, and recharging your touristic batteries. Slow down and be open to unexpected experiences and the hospitality of the Bavarian people.

Sip a stein of beer while men in lederhosen play oompah music, take a joy ride on a bike through the English Garden, or head into the Alps and climb to a fairy-tale castle. As you visit places I know and love, I'm happy you'll be meeting some of my favorite Germans.

Happy travels! *Gute Reise!*

Munich City Walk

Munich is big and modern, but with its pedestrian-friendly historic core, it feels a lot like an easygoing Bavarian town. On this self-guided walk, we'll start in the central square, see its famous glockenspiel, stroll through a thriving open-air market, and visit historic churches with lavish Baroque decor. We'll stop at a venerable gourmet deli and take a spin through the world's most famous beer hall. Allow two to three hours for this walk through a thousand years of Munich's history. Allow extra time if you tour museums along the way.

Though Munich is the modern capital of Bavaria and a major metropolis, its low-key atmosphere has led Germans to dub it *Millionendorf*—the "village of a million people."

ORIENTATION

New Town Hall: The glockenspiel performs daily at 11:00 and 12:00 all year (10-minute show; also at 17:00 March-Oct). The elevator to the tower is €3 and runs daily 10:00-19:00; Oct-April Mon-Fri 10:00-17:00, closed Sat-Sun (elevator located under glockenspiel).

St. Peter's Church Tower Climb: €5, daily 12:00-16:30.

Viktualienmarkt: Mon-Sat from morning until evening, closed Sun.

Munich City Museum: €4, Tue-Sun 10:00-18:00, closed Mon.

Asam Church: Free, Sat-Thu 9:00-19:00, Fri from 13:00, no entry during Mass.

St. Michael's Church: Church—free to enter, generally daily 8:00-19:00, closes later on Sun and summer evenings; crypt—€2, Mon-Fri 9:30-16:30, Sat until 14:30, closed Sun; frequent concerts—check posted schedule; +49 89 231 7060.

Frauenkirche: Free, generally daily 7:00-20:30; church towers—€6, +49 89 290 0820.

Dallmayr Delicatessen: Mon-Sat 9:30-19:00, closed Sun.

Hofbräuhaus: Free to enter, daily 9:00-late, live oompah music at lunch and dinner.

Other Eateries: Recommendations for eateries along this walk can be found on page 112.

Tours: ∩ Download my free Munich City Walk audio tour.

THE WALK BEGINS

▶ *Begin your walk at the heart of the old city, with a stroll through...*

❶ Marienplatz

Riding the escalator out of the subway into sunlit Marienplatz (mah-REE-en-platz, "Mary's Square") gives you a fine first look at the glory of Munich: great buildings, outdoor cafés, and people bustling and lingering like the birds and breeze with which they share this square.

The square is both old and new: For a thousand years, it's been the center of Munich. It was the town's marketplace and public forum, standing at a crossroads along the Salt Road, which ran between Salzburg and Augsburg.

Lining one entire side of the square is the impressive facade of the **New Town Hall** (Neues Rathaus), with its soaring 280-foot spire. The structure looks medieval, but it was actually built in the late 1800s (1867-1908). The style is Neo-Gothic—pointed arches over the doorways and a roofline bristling with prickly spires. The 40 statues look like medieval saints, but they're from around 1900, depicting more recent Bavarian kings and nobles. This medieval-looking style was all the rage in the 19th century as Germans were rediscovering their historical roots and uniting as a modern nation.

The New Town Hall is famous for its **glockenspiel.** A carillon in the tower chimes a tune while colorful figurines come out on the balcony to spin and dance. The *Spiel* of the glockenspiel tells the story of a noble wedding that took place on the market square in 1568. You see the wedding procession and the friendly joust of knights on horseback. The duke and his bride watch the action as the groom's Bavarian family (in Bavarian white and blue) joyfully jousts with the bride's French family (in red and white). Below, the barrelmakers—famous for being the first to dance in the streets after a deadly plague lifted—do their popular jig. Finally, the solitary cock crows.

At the very top of the New Town Hall is a statue of a child with outstretched arms, dressed in monk's garb and holding a book in its left hand. This is the **Münchner Kindl,** the symbol of Munich. The town got its name from the people who first settled here: the monks (*Mönchen*). You'll spot this mini monk all over town, on everything from the city's coat of arms to souvenir shot glasses to ad campaigns (often holding not a book but maybe a beer or a smartphone). The city symbol was originally depicted as a grown man, wearing a gold-lined black cloak and red shoes. By the 19th century, artists were

The glockenspiel show at New Town Hall...

...features colorful figurines that spin and dance.

Munich City Walk

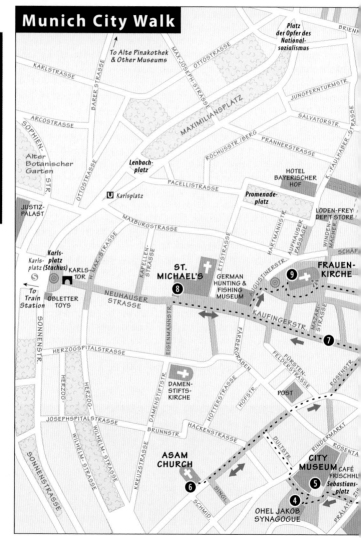

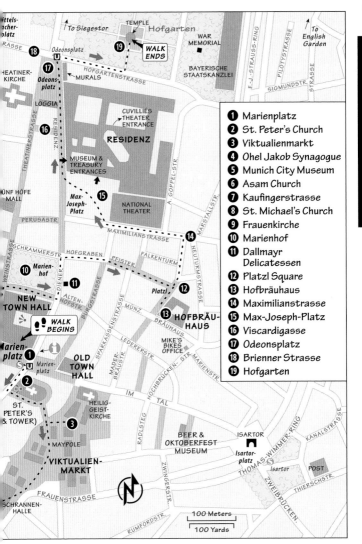

To Siegestor
TEMPLE
Hofgarten
WAR MEMORIAL
To English Garden
WALK ENDS
BAYERISCHE STAATSKANZLEI
Odeonsplatz
HOFGARTENSTRASSE
MURALS
THEATINER-KIRCHE
LOGGIA
CUVILLIES THEATER ENTRANCE
RESIDENZ
MÜNF HÖFE MALL
MUSEUM & TREASURY ENTRANCES
Max-Joseph-Platz
NATIONAL THEATER
PERUSASTR.
MAXIMILIANSTRASSE
HOFGRABEN
Marienhof
FALKENTURM
NEW TOWN HALL
PFISTER
Platzl
WALK BEGINS
HOFBRÄU-HAUS
BRÄUHAUS
Marienplatz
OLD TOWN HALL
MIKE'S BIKES OFFICE
ST. PETER'S & TOWER)
HEILIG-GEIST-KIRCHE
VIKTUALIEN-MARKT
MAYPOLE
BEER & OKTOBERFEST MUSEUM
ISARTOR
Isartorplatz
Isartor
POST
SCHRANNEN-HALLE
FRAUENSTRASSE
N
100 Meters
100 Yards

1 Marienplatz
2 St. Peter's Church
3 Viktualienmarkt
4 Ohel Jakob Synagogue
5 Munich City Museum
6 Asam Church
7 Kaufingerstrasse
8 St. Michael's Church
9 Frauenkirche
10 Marienhof
11 Dallmayr Delicatessen
12 Platzl Square
13 Hofbräuhaus
14 Maximilianstrasse
15 Max-Joseph-Platz
16 Viscardigasse
17 Odeonsplatz
18 Brienner Strasse
19 Hofgarten

representing him as a young boy, then a gender-neutral child, and, more recently, a young girl.

These days, a teenage girl dressed as the *Kindl* kicks off the annual Oktoberfest by leading the opening parade on horseback, and then serves as the mascot throughout the festivities.

For great **views** of the city, you can ride an elevator to the fourth floor (where you purchase your ticket), then ride another elevator to the top of the New Town Hall tower—where, from a small perch, you can enjoy a commanding 360-degree city view.

The **golden statue** at the top of the column in the center of Marienplatz honors the square's namesake, the Virgin Mary. Sculpted in 1590, it was a rallying point in the religious wars of the Reformation. Back then, Munich was a bastion of southern-German Catholicism against the heresies of Martin Luther to the north. Notice how, at the four corners of the statue, cherubs fight the four great biblical enemies of civilization: the dragon of war, the lion of hunger, the rooster-headed monster of plague and disease, and the serpent. The serpent represents heresy—namely, Protestants. Bavaria is still Catholic country, and Protestants weren't allowed to worship openly here until about 1800.

To the right of the New Town Hall, the gray pointy building with the green spires is the **Old Town Hall** (Altes Rathaus). On its adjoining bell tower, find the city seal. It has the Münchner Kindl (symbolizing the first monks), a castle (representing the first fortifications), and a lion (representing the first ruler—Henry the Lion, who built them). It was in this building, on November 9, 1938, that Hitler called for Germans to rise up and ransack everything Jewish. On what came to be called Kristallnacht, synagogues were burned and shops were trashed. (Inside the tunnel under the building is a memorial plaque recalling this horrible event, which foreshadowed the Holocaust.)

As you look around, keep in mind that the Allies bombed Marienplatz and much of Munich during World War II. Most of the buildings had to be rebuilt; the question was whether to do so in a way that matched their original design or in a modern style. The Old Town Hall looks newer now because it was destroyed by bombs and was rebuilt after the war. The New Town Hall survived the bombs, and served as the US military headquarters after the Americans occupied Munich in 1945.

The New Town Hall tower dominates—and a golden statue anchors—Marienplatz.

Before moving on, face the New Town Hall one more time and get oriented. Straight ahead is north. To the left is the pedestrian shopping street called Kaufingerstrasse, which leads to the old gate called Karlstor and the train station. To the right, the street leads to the Isartor gate and the Deutsches Museum. This east-west axis cuts through the historic core of Munich.

▶ *Turn around and notice the small street to the left leading a short block to St. Peter's Church, with its steeple poking up above a row of buildings.*

❷ St. Peter's Church

The oldest church in town, St. Peter's stands on the hill where Munich's original monks probably settled—perhaps as far back as the ninth century (although the city marks its official birthday as 1158). Today's church (from 1368) replaced the original monastery church. St. Peter's ("Old Peter" to locals) is part of the soul of the city. There's even a popular song about it that goes, "Munich is not Munich without St. Peter's."

Step inside. If there's no Mass, feel free to explore. Typical of so many Bavarian churches, it's whitewashed and light-filled, with highlights in pastel pinks and blues framed by gold curlicues. The ceiling painting opens up to the heavens, where Peter is crucified upside down.

Photos (on a pillar near the entrance) show how St. Peter's was badly damaged in World War II: The roof caved in, and the tower was demolished during an air raid. But the beloved church was rebuilt and restored. The nave is lined with bronze statues of the apostles, and the altar shows a statue of St. Peter being adored by four Church

St. Peter's tower has great views.

Inside the church is Munditia, a saint in a box.

fathers. The precious and fragile sandstone Gothic chapel altar (to the left of the main altar) survived the war only because it was buried in sandbags.

Find the second chapel from the back on the left side. Now there's something you don't see every day: a skeleton in a box. As the red Latin inscription says, this is St. Munditia. In the fourth century, she was beheaded by the Romans for her Christian faith. Munich has more relics of saints than any city outside Rome. That's because it was the pope's Catholic bastion against the rising tide of Protestantism in northern Europe during the Reformation. In 1675, St. Munditia's remains were given to Munich by the pope as thanks for the city's devoted service.

▶ *Leave St. Peter's out the door opposite the one you entered. Then, head to the right to the tower entrance.*

It's a long climb to the top (306 steps, no elevator, can be hot and sweaty in summer), much of it with two-way traffic on a one-lane staircase—but the view is rewarding. Try to be two flights from the top when the bells ring at the top of the hour. Then, when your friends back home ask you about your trip, you'll say, "What?"

▶ *After your tower climb, head downhill to join the busy commotion of the...*

❸ Viktualienmarkt

The market is a lively world of produce stands and budget eateries. Browse your way through the stalls and pavilions, as you make your way to the market's main landmark, the white-and-blue-striped maypole. Early in the morning, you can still feel small-town Munich here. Remember, Munich has been a market town since its earliest days as a stop on the salt-trade crossroads. By the 1400s, the market bustled, most likely beneath a traditional maypole, just like you see today.

Besides salt, Munich gained a reputation for beer. By the 15th century, more than 30 breweries pumped out the golden liquid, brewed by monks, who were licensed to sell it. They stored their beer in cellars under courtyards kept cool by the shade of bushy chestnut trees—a tradition Munich's breweries still practice.

Today, the market's centerpiece seems to be its **beer garden,** with picnic tables in the shade of chestnut trees. Shoppers pause here for a late-morning snack of *Weisswurst*—white sausage—served with mustard, a pretzel, and a beer. As is the tradition at all the city's beer

The History of Munich

Born from Salt and Beer (1100-1500): Munich began in the 12th century, when Henry the Lion established a lucrative salt trade near a monastery of "monks"—München. After Henry's death, an ambitious merchant family, the Wittelsbachs, took over. By the 1400s, Munich's maypole-studded market bustled with trade in salt and beer, the twin-domed Frauenkirche drew pilgrims, and the Wittelsbachs made their home in the Residenz. When the various regions of Bavaria united in 1506, Munich (pop. 14,000) was the natural capital.

Religious Wars, Plagues, Decline (1500-1800): While Martin Luther and the Protestant Reformation raged in northern Germany, Munich became the ultra-Catholic heart of the Counter-Reformation, decorated in the ornate Baroque and Rococo style of its Italian Catholic allies. The religious wars and periodic plagues left the city weakened. Now the Wittelsbachs took their cultural cues from more-powerful France (Nymphenburg Palace is a miniature Versailles), England (the English Garden), and Italy (the Pitti Palace-inspired Residenz). While the rest of Europe modernized, Munich remained behind the times.

The Golden Age of Kings (1806-1886): When Napoleon invaded, the Wittelsbach dukes surrendered hospitably and were promptly rewarded with an even grander title: King of Bavaria. Munich boomed. **Maximilian I** (r. 1806-1825), a.k.a. Max Joseph, rebuilt in Neoclassical style—grand columned buildings connected by broad boulevards. **Ludwig I** (r. 1825-1848) turned Munich into a modern railroad hub, budding industrial city, and fitting capital (pop. 90,000). But the skirt-chasing Ludwig was brought down in a sex scandal with the notorious Irish dancer Lola Montez. His son **Maximilian II** (r. 1848-1864) continued

Ludwig's modernization program, while studiously avoiding dancers. In 1864, 18-year-old **Ludwig II** (r. 1864-1886) became king. Ludwig didn't much like Munich, preferring to build castles in the Bavarian countryside. (For more on Ludwig, see page 130.)

End of the Wittelsbachs (1886-1918): When Bavaria became part of the newly united Germany, Berlin overtook Munich as Germany's power center. Turn-of-the-century Munich was culturally rich, giving birth to the abstract art of the Blue Rider group. But World War I devastated Munich. After the war, mobs of poor, hungry, disillusioned, and angry Münchners roamed the streets. In 1918, they drove the last Bavarian king out, ending 700 years of Wittelsbach rule.

Nazis, World War II, and Munich Bombed (1918-1945): In the power vacuum, a fringe group emerged—the Nazi Party, headed by charismatic war veteran Adolf Hitler. Hitler rallied the Nazis in a Munich beer hall, leading a failed coup d'état known as the Beer Hall Putsch (1923). When the Nazis eventually took power in Berlin, they remembered their roots, dubbing Munich "Capital of the Movement." In World War II, nearly half the city was leveled by Allied air raids. The once-grand city lay in waste.

Munich Rebuilds (1945-Present): After the war, with generous American aid, Münchners rebuilt. Nazi authorities had taken care during the early war years to create a photographic archive of historic sights, which now came in handy. The city faced a choice—rebuild in the old style or go with modern skyscrapers. Munich chose to preserve the low-rise, medieval feel, but with a modern infrastructure. For the 1972 Olympic Games, they built a futuristic stadium, a sleek new subway system, and one of Europe's first pedestrian-only zones—Kaufingerstrasse. In 1990, when Germany reunited, Berlin once again became the country's focal point, relegating Munich to the role of sleepy Second City.

These days, Munich seems to be comfortable just being itself rather than trying to keep up with Berlin. Though rich and modern—home to BMW and Siemens, and a producer of software, books, movies, and the latest fashions—it remains safe, clean, and cultured. It's a university town, built on a human scale, and close to the beauties of nature.

The Viktualienmarkt sells fresh produce, gourmet foods, and beer to a people-watching crowd.

gardens, some tables—those without tablecloths—are set aside for patrons who bring their own food, as long as they buy a drink.

The towering **maypole,** colorfully ornamented, is typical of Bavaria's town squares. Many are painted, like this one, in Bavaria's colors, white and blue. The decorations are festively replaced every year on the first of May. Traditionally, rival communities try to steal each other's maypole. Locals guard their new pole day and night as May Day approaches. Stolen poles are ransomed only with lots of beer for the clever thieves.

As was standard in any village, the decorations that line each side of the pole explain which merchants are doing business in the market. Munich's maypole gives prominence (on the bottom level) to a horse-drawn wagon bringing in beer barrels. And you can't have a kegger without coopers—the dancing barrelmakers. The bottom of the pole celebrates the world's oldest food law. The German Beer Purity Law (*Reinheitsgebot*) of 1487 originated here in Munich, was later adopted in Bavaria, and eventually spread throughout the rest of Germany. It stipulated that beer could consist only of three ingredients: barley, hops, and water, with no additives. (Later they realized that a fourth ingredient, yeast, is always present in fermentation.) Why was beer so treasured? Back in the Middle Ages, it was considered liquid food.

From the maypole, take in the bustling scene around you. The market was modernized in the 1800s as the city grew. Today, this traditional market (sitting on the city's most expensive real estate) survives thanks to a ban on fast-food chains and city laws that favor old-time shops with low taxes. Münchners consider the produce here to be top quality, if on the expensive side.

▶ *At the bottom end of the Viktualienmarkt, cross the street and continue to a modern glass-and-iron building, the* **Schrannenhalle.** *Stroll through this high-end mall of deli shops (in a former 1800s grain hall) to the far end, where wine connoisseurs could detour downstairs for a vast wine collection.*

Exit the Schrannenhalle midway down on the right-hand side. You'll spill out into **Sebastiansplatz,** *a small square lined with healthy eateries. Continue through Sebastiansplatz and veer left, where you'll see a cube-shaped building, the...*

❹ Ohel Jakob Synagogue

This modern synagogue anchors a revitalized Jewish quarter. In the 1930s, about 10,000 Jews lived in Munich, and the main synagogue stood near here (on Karlsplatz). Then, in 1938, Hitler demanded that the synagogue be torn down. By the end of World War II, Munich's Jewish community was gone. But thanks to Germany's later acceptance of religious refugees from former Soviet states, the Jewish population (while mostly secular) has now reached its prewar size. The new synagogue was built in 2006. There's also a kindergarten and day school, playground, fine

The market's maypole depicts a beer wagon.   Ohel Jakob Synagogue evokes the Wailing Wall.

kosher restaurant (at #18), and bookstore. Notice the low-key but efficient security.

While the synagogue is shut tight to nonworshippers, its architecture is striking from the outside. Lower stones of travertine evoke the Wailing Wall in Jerusalem, while an upper section represents the tent that held important religious wares during the 40 years of wandering through the desert. The synagogue's door features the first 10 letters of the Hebrew alphabet, symbolizing the Ten Commandments.

▶ *Facing the synagogue, on the same square, is the worthwhile* ❺ *Munich City Museum (Münchner Stadtmuseum), described on page 84. Continue through the synagogue's square, past the fountain, across the street, and one block farther to the pedestrianized Sendlinger Strasse. Take a left and walk 100 yards until you see the fancy facade on the right marking the...*

❻ Asam Church (Asamkirche)

This tiny church is a slice of heaven on earth—a gooey, drippy Baroque-concentrate masterpiece by Bavaria's top two Rococonuts—the Asam brothers. Just 30 feet wide, it was built in 1740 to fit within this row of homes. Originally, it was a private chapel where these two brother-architects could show off their work (on their own land, next to their home and business headquarters—to the left), but it's now a public place of worship.

This place of worship served as a promotional brochure to woo clients and is packed with every architectural trick in the books. Imagine approaching the church not as a worshipper but as a shopper representing your church's building committee. First stand outside: Hmmm, the look of those foundation stones really packs a punch. And the legs hanging over the portico...nice effect. Those starbursts on the door would be a hit back home, too.

Then step inside: I'll take a set of those over-the-top golden capitals, please. We'd also like to order the gilded garlands draping the church in jubilation, and the twin cupids capping the confessional. And how about some fancy stucco work, too? Check out the illusion of a dome painted on the flat ceiling—that'll save us lots of money. The yellow glass above the altar has the effect of the thin-sliced alabaster at St. Peter's in Rome, but it's within our budget! And, tapping the "marble" pilasters to determine that they are just painted fakes, we

The Asam Church is drenched from top to bottom with curves, corkscrew columns, and cupids.

decide to take that, too. Crammed between two buildings, this narrow church has limited light inside, so there's a big, clear window in the back for maximum illumination—we'll order one to cut back on our electricity bill.

Visiting the Asam Church, you can see why the prolific Asam brothers were so successful. (Black-and-white portraits of the two Asams in oval frames flank the altar.) On the way out, say goodbye to the gilded grim reaper in the narthex (above, on the left side, as you're leaving) as he cuts the thread of life.

▶ *Leaving the church, look to your right, noticing the Sendlinger Tor at the end of the street—part of the fortified town wall that circled Munich in the 14th century. Then turn left and walk straight up Sendlinger Strasse. Walk toward the spire of the New Town Hall in the distance, and then up (pedestrian-only) Rosenstrasse, until you hit Marienplatz and the big, busy...*

❼ Kaufingerstrasse

This car-free street leads you through a great shopping district, past cheap department stores, carnivals of street entertainers, and good old-fashioned slicers and dicers. As far back as the 12th century, this was the town's main commercial street. Traders from Salzburg and Augsburg would enter the town through the fortified Karlstor. This street led past the Augustiner beer hall (opposite St. Michael's Church to this day), right to the main square and cathedral.

Up until the 1970s, the street was jammed with car traffic. Then, for the 1972 Olympics, it was turned into one of Europe's first pedestrian zones. At first, shopkeepers were afraid that would ruin business. Now it's Munich's living room. Nearly 9,000 shoppers pass through it each hour. Merchants nearby are begging for their streets to become traffic-free, too.

Munich has become one of the globe's greenest cities. Skyscrapers have been banished to the suburbs, and the nearby Frauenkirche is still the tallest building in the center.

▶ *Stroll a few blocks away from Marienplatz toward the Karlstor, until you arrive at the imposing church on the right.*

❽ St. Michael's Church (Michaelskirche)

This is one of the first great Renaissance buildings north of the Alps. The ornate facade, with its sloped roofline, was inspired by the Gesù Church in Rome—home of the Jesuit order. Jesuits saw themselves as the intellectual defenders of Catholicism. St. Michael's was built in the late 1500s—at the height of the Protestant Reformation—to serve as the northern outpost of the Jesuits. Appropriately, the facade features a statue of Michael fighting a Protestant demon.

Inside, admire the ornate Baroque interior, topped with a barrel vault, the largest of its day. Stroll up the nave to the ornate pulpit,

Kaufingerstrasse—traffic-free shopping

St. Michael's—a bastion of the Jesuits

where Jesuit priests would hammer away at Reformation heresy. The church's acoustics are spectacular, and the choir—famous in Munich—sounds heavenly singing from the organ loft high in the rear. Notice the monochrome Baroque of the all-white interior (with only shadows to "color" the surfaces) and the lavish chapels lining each side (some of which were built by and for local leading families and came with a promise from the priests that their privileged loved ones would get special prayers daily).

The crypt (*Fürstengruft,* down the stairs to the right by the altar) contains 40 stark, somewhat forlorn tombs of Bavaria's ruling family, the Wittelsbachs. The most ornate tomb (center of back wall, facing altar) holds the illustrious Ludwig II, known for his fairy-tale castle at Neuschwanstein. Ludwig spent his days building castles, listening to music, and dreaming about knights of old. His excesses earned him the nickname "Mad" King Ludwig. But of all the Wittelsbachs, it's his tomb that's decorated with flowers—placed here by romantics still mad about their "mad" king.

▶ *Backtrack a couple of blocks up Kaufingerstrasse to the wild boar statue. At the boar statue, turn left on Augustinerstrasse, which leads to Munich's towering, twin-domed cathedral, the...*

❾ Frauenkirche

These twin onion domes are the symbol of the city. They're unusual in that most Gothic churches have either pointed steeples or square towers. Some say Crusaders, inspired by the Dome of the Rock in Jerusalem, brought home the idea (first to St. Mark's in Venice and then north of the Alps). Or it may be that, due to money problems, the towers weren't completed until Renaissance times, when domes were in vogue. Whatever the reason, the Frauenkirche's domes may be the inspiration for the characteristic domed church spires that mark villages all over Bavaria.

The church was built in just 22 years, from 1466 to 1488. Note that it's made of brick, not quarried stone—easy to make locally, and cheaper and faster to build with than stone. Construction was partly funded with the sale of indulgences (which let sinners bypass purgatory on the way to heaven). It's dedicated to the Virgin—Our Lady (*Frau*)—and has been the city's cathedral since 1821.

▶ *Step inside and remember that much of this church was destroyed*

The Frauenkirche's twin onion domes are the city's most recognizable landmark.

during World War II. The towers survived, and the rest was rebuilt essentially from scratch.

Near the entrance is a big, black, ornate, tomb-like monument honoring Ludwig IV the Bavarian (1282-1347), who was elected Holy Roman Emperor—a big deal. The Frauenkirche was built a century later with the express purpose of honoring his memory.

Nearby, a relief (over the back pew on the left) honors one of Munich's more recent citizens. Joseph Ratzinger (1927-2022) was born in Bavaria, became archbishop of the Frauenkirche (1977-1982), then moved to the Vatican, where he later served as Pope Benedict XVI (2005-2013).

Now walk slowly up the main aisle, enjoying stained glass right and left. This glass is obviously modern, having replaced the original glass that was shattered in World War II. Ahead is the high altar, under a huge hanging crucifix. Find the throne—the ceremonial seat of the local bishop. From here, look up to the tops of the columns, and notice the tiny painted portraits. They're the craftsmen from five centuries ago who helped build the church.

Now walk behind the altar to the apse, where the three tall windows still have their original 15th-century glass. To survive the bombs of 1944, each pane was lovingly removed and stored safely away.

Leaving the church, walk up its right side. Notice the 16th- and 17th-century tombstones on the wall. Originally, people were buried in the holy ground around the church. But in the Napoleonic age, the cemeteries were dug up and relocated outside the city walls for hygienic and space reasons. They kept a few tombstones here as a reminder of this heritage.

Also take a closer look at the towering church's patchwork of old and new bricks. After World War II, legions of "rubble women" cleaned up the devastation in bombed-out Munich. Broken bricks were set aside and used to build the city's *Schuttberge,* or "debris hills," which are now grassy parks at the edge of town. Intact bricks were cleaned and reused in rebuilding.

▶ *At the rear of the church, go down Filserbräugasse and cross Weinstrasse. Look left, and you'll see a construction zone, which is normally a green park called the Marienhof.*

Oktoberfest

Munich hosts the planet's biggest kegger—Oktoberfest. It first happened in 1810, when King Ludwig I's wedding reception was such a rousing success that they decided to do it again the next year. And the next, and the next...

These days, Oktoberfest lasts just more than two weeks, starting on a Saturday in September and usually ending on the first Sunday in October. It's held at the Theresienwiese fairground south of the main train station, in a meadow known as the "Wies'n" (VEE-zen). They set up huge tents that together can seat nearly 120,000 beer drinkers. The festivities kick off with an opening parade. Then, for the next two weeks, it's a frenzy of drinking, dancing, music, and food. There's a huge Ferris wheel. The triple-loop roller coaster must be the wildest on earth. (Best done before the beer-drinking.) Total strangers stroll arm-in-arm down rows of picnic tables amid a carnival of beer, pretzels, and wurst, drawing visitors from all over the globe. A million gallons of beer later, they roast the last ox.

⑩ Marienhof

This square, tucked behind the New Town Hall, was left as a green island after the 1945 bombings. For now, the square's all dug up while Munich builds an additional subway tunnel. With virtually the entire underground system converging on nearby Marienplatz, this new tunnel will provide a huge relief to the city's congested subterranean infrastructure. Billboards on the site show what's going on underground; in a few years the massive new subway station will open and this will once again be a park.

▶ *On the far side of Marienhof, the stately yellow building is...*

⑪ Dallmayr Delicatessen

When the king wanted take-out, he called Alois Dallmayr. This place became famous for its exotic and luxurious food items: tropical fruits, seafood, chocolates, fine wines, and coffee (there are meat and cheese counters, too). As you enter, read the black plaque with the royal seal by the door: *Königlich Bayerischer Hof-Lieferant* ("Deliverer for the King of Bavaria and his Court"). Catering to royal and aristocratic tastes (and budgets) since 1700, it's still the choice of Munich's old rich. Today, it's most famous for its sweets, chocolates, and coffee—dispensed from fine hand-painted Nymphenburg porcelain jugs.

▶ *Leaving Dallmayr, turn right and then right again to continue along Hofgraben. Walk straight three blocks, gently downhill, to Platzl—"small square." (If you get turned around, just ask any local to point you toward the Hofbräuhaus.)*

⑫ Platzl Square

As you stand here—admiring classic facades in the heart of medieval Munich—recall that everything around you was flattened in World War II. Here (and throughout the city), reconstruction happened in stages: From 1945 to 1950, they removed 12 million tons of bricks and replaced roofs to make buildings weathertight. From 1950 to 1972, they redid the exteriors. From 1972 to 2000, they refurbished the interiors. Today, the rebuilt Platzl sports new—but old-looking—facades.

Officials estimate that hundreds of unexploded bombs still lie buried under Munich. As recently as 2012, a 550-pound bomb was found in Schwabing, a neighborhood just north of the old city center. They had to evacuate the neighborhood and detonate the bomb, which created a huge fireball—a stark reminder of Munich's scary past.

Assemble an aristocratic picnic at Dallmayr.

Platzl Square—post-war rebuild

Today's Platzl hosts a lively mix of places to eat and drink—chains like Starbucks and Hard Rock Café alongside local spots like Schuhbecks Eissalon, a favorite for ice cream (Pfisterstrasse 11).

▶ *At the bottom of the square (#9), you can experience the venerable...*

⓭ Hofbräuhaus

The world's most famous beer hall is a trip. Whether or not you slide your lederhosen on its polished benches, it's a great experience just to walk through the place in all its rowdy glory.

Before going in, check out the huge arches at the entrance and the crown logo. The original brewery was built here in 1589. As the crown suggests, it was the Wittelsbachs' personal brewery, to make the "court brew" (*Hof Brau*). In 1880, the brewery moved out, and this 5,000-seat food-and-beer palace was built in its place. After being bombed in World War II, the Hofbräuhaus was one of the first places to be rebuilt (Bavarian priorities).

Now take a deep breath and go on in. Dive headlong into the sudsy Hofbräu mosh pit. Don't be shy. Everyone's drunk anyway. The atmosphere is thick with the sounds of oompah music, played here every night of the year.

You'll see locals stuffed into lederhosen and dirndls, giant gingerbread cookies that sport romantic messages, and kiosks selling goofy postcards. You'll see signs on some tables reading *Stammtisch,* meaning they're reserved for regulars, and their racks of old beer steins made of pottery and pewter. A slogan on the ceiling above the band reads, *Durst ist schlimmer als Heimweh*—"Thirst is worse than homesickness."

You can explore upstairs, too. Next to the entrance, a grand staircase leads up to the big folk-show hall on the top floor. If you don't

The Hofbräuhaus—a tradition since 1880

Music plays every day at the Hofbräuhaus.

mind eating with 20 big-bus tours, this can be a cheap and fun way to see a slap dancing and yodeling show.

▶ *Leaving the Hofbräuhaus, turn right and walk two blocks, then turn left when you reach the busy street called...*

⓮ Maximilianstrasse

This broad east-west boulevard, lined with grand buildings and exclusive shops, introduces us to Munich's golden age of the 1800s. In that period, Bavaria was ruled by three important kings: Max Joseph, Ludwig I, and Ludwig II. They transformed Munich from a cluster of medieval lanes to a modern city of spacious squares, Neoclassical monuments, and wide boulevards. At the east end of this boulevard is the palatial home of the Bavarian parliament.

The street was purposely designed for shopping. And to this day, it has Munich's most exclusive shops. Many shoppers are wealthy visitors from the Middle East, here for medical treatment or vacation.

▶ *Maximilianstrasse leads to a big square—Max-Joseph-Platz.*

⓯ Max-Joseph-Platz

The square is fronted by two big buildings: the National Theater (with its columns) and the Residenz (with its intimidating stone facade).

The **Residenz,** the former "residence" of the royal Wittelsbach family, started as a crude castle (c. 1385). Over the centuries, it evolved into one of Europe's most opulent palaces. The facade takes its cue from the Pitti Palace in Florence. Today, you can visit the Residenz for its lavish Rococo interior, crown jewels, and exquisite Cuvilliés Theater (all described in the Residenz Tour chapter).

The square's centerpiece is a grand statue of **Maximilian I**—a.k.a. Max Joseph. In 1806, Max was the city's duke, serving in the long tradition of his Wittelsbach family...until Napoleon invaded and deposed him. But then Napoleon—eager to marry into the aristocracy—agreed to reinstate Max, with one condition: that his daughter marry Napoleon's stepson. Max Joseph agreed, and was quickly crowned not duke but king of Bavaria.

Max Joseph and his heirs ruled as constitutional monarchs. Now a king, Max Joseph was popular; he emancipated Protestants and Jews, revamped the Viktualienmarkt, and graced Munich with grand buildings like the **National Theater.** This Neoclassical building, opened in

Max Joseph welcomes you to Max-Joseph-Platz, home to the National Theater and Residenz.

1818, celebrated Bavaria's strong culture, deep roots, and legitimacy as a nation; four of Richard Wagner's operas were first performed here. It's now where the Bavarian State Opera and the Bavarian State Orchestra perform. (The Roman numerals MCMLXIII in the frieze mark the year the theater reopened after WWII bombing restoration—1963.)

▶ *Leave Max-Joseph-Platz opposite where you entered, walking alongside the Residenz palace on Residenzstrasse. Pause at the first corner on the left and look down Viscardigasse at the gold-cobbled swoosh in the pavement.*

🄻 Viscardigasse

The cobbles in Viscardigasse recall one of Munich's most dramatic moments: It was 1923, and Munich was in chaos. World War I had left Germany in shambles. Angry mobs roamed the streets. Out of the fury rose a new and frightening movement—Adolf Hitler and the Nazi Party. On November 8, Hitler launched a coup, later known as the Beer Hall Putsch, to try to topple the German government. It started with a fiery speech by Hitler in a beer hall a few blocks from here (the beer hall no longer exists). The next day, Hitler and his mob of Nazis marched up Residenzstrasse. A block ahead, where Residenzstrasse spills into Odeonsplatz, stood a hundred government police. Shots were fired. Hitler was injured, and 16 Nazis were killed, along with four policemen. The coup was put down, and Hitler was sent to a prison outside Munich. During his nine months there, he wrote down his twisted ideas in his book *Mein Kampf.*

Ten years later, when Hitler finally came to power, he made a memorial at Odeonsplatz to honor the "first martyrs of the Third Reich." Germans were required to raise their arms in a Sieg Heil salute as they entered the square. The only way to avoid the indignity of saluting Nazism was to turn left down Viscardigasse instead. That stream of shiny cobbles marks the detour taken by those brave dissenters.

▶ *But now that Hitler's odious memorial is long gone, you can continue to…*

⓱ Odeonsplatz

This square links Munich's illustrious past with the Munich of today. It was laid out by the Wittelsbach kings in the 1800s. They incorporated the much older (yellow) church that was already on the square, the Theatinerkirche. This church contains about half of the Wittelsbach tombs. The church's twin towers and 230-foot-high dome are classic Italian Baroque, reflecting Munich's strong Catholic bent in the 1600s.

Overlooking the square from the south is an arcaded loggia filled with statues. In the 1800s the Wittelsbachs commissioned this Hall of Heroes to honor Bavarian generals. It was modeled after the famous Renaissance loggia in Florence. Odeonsplatz was part of the Wittelsbachs' grand vision of modern urban planning, designed to connect the historic core with the expanding metropolis.

At the far end of the square, several wide boulevards lead away from here. Look west (left) down ⓲ **Brienner Strasse,** which (though it's not visible from here) leads to Königsplatz, the Museum Quarter, and, a few miles beyond, the Wittelsbachs' impressive summer home, Nymphenburg Palace.

The boulevard heading north from Odeonsplatz is **Ludwigstrasse.** It stretches a full mile, flanked by an impressive line of uniform 60-foot-tall buildings in the Neo-Renaissance style. In the far distance is the city's Triumphal Arch, the Siegestor, capped with a figure of Bavaria, a goddess riding a lion-drawn chariot. She's looking out, away from the city, to welcome home returning soldiers. The street is named for the

In 1923, Hitler launched a failed coup that drew huge crowds to Marienplatz.

great Wittelsbach builder-king Ludwig I, the grandfather of "Mad" King Ludwig. It was Ludwig I who truly made Munich into a grand capital. ("I won't rest," he famously swore, "until Munich looks like Athens.") The street that bears his name, Ludwigstrasse, was used for big parades and processions, as it leads to that Roman-style arch.

Beyond the arch—and beyond what you can see—lie the suburbs of modern Munich, including the city's modern skyscrapers, Olympic Park, and the famous BMW headquarters.

As you enjoy the busy scene on Odeonsplatz, let's bring Munich's 850-year history up to the present. Munich today, with a population of 1.5 million, is Germany's third-largest city, after Berlin and Hamburg. It's the capital of the independent-minded German state of Bavaria, and proudly waves two flags: the white-and-blue diamonds of Bavaria and the black-and-gold of the city of Munich. Munich is home to more banks and financial firms than any German city besides Frankfurt. It's a center for book publishing and TV production. Information technology is big, as well: Munich is home to electronics giant Siemens and the German branch of Microsoft. And, of course, Munich is home to the manufacturer of some of the world's finest cars—BMW

41

(*Bayerische Motoren Werke,* "Bavarian Motor Works"). Yes, Munich is a major metropolis, but you'd hardly know it by walking through the pleasant streets and parks of "Millionendorf."

▶ *We'll finish our walk in the pleasant Hofgarten. Its formal gate is to your right as you're facing up Ludwigstrasse. Step through the gate and enter the...*

⑲ Hofgarten

The elegant "garden of the royal court" is a delight. Built by the Wittelsbachs as their own private backyard to the Residenz palace, it's now open to everyone. Just inside the gate is an arcade decorated with murals commissioned by Ludwig I in the early 1800s. While faded, they still tell the glorious story of Bavaria from 1155 until 1688. The garden's 400-year-old centerpiece is a Renaissance-style temple with great acoustics. It's decorated with the same shell decor as was popular inside the Residenz.

▶ *You've seen the essential Munich and are within easy reach of the city's top sights. From here, to reach the English Garden, angle downhill to the northeast, walk under a bridge, and then make your way to Von-der-Tann-Strasse, the main street that runs just north of the Hofgarten.*

The Hofgarten, the former royal garden, is the gateway to the even-larger English Garden.

MUNICH CITY WALK

The Residenz Tour

For 500 years, this was the palatial "residence" and seat of power of the ruling Wittelsbach family. It began (1385) as a crude castle with a moat around it. The main building was built from 1550 to 1650 and decorated in Rococo style during the 18th century. The final touch (under Ludwig I) was the grand south facade modeled after Florence's Pitti Palace. In March 1944, Allied air raids left the Residenz in shambles, so much of what we see today—like much of historic Munich—is a reconstruction.

The vast Residenz complex is divided into three sections: The **Residenz Museum** is a long hike through 90 lavishly decorated rooms. The **Residenz Treasury** shows off the Wittelsbach crown jewels. The **Cuvilliés Theater** is an ornate Rococo opera house. While each has its own admission, the combo-ticket saves money if you're doing all three.

ORIENTATION

Cost: Residenz Museum—€9, Residenz Treasury—€9 (both include essential audioguides), Cuvilliés Theater—€5; the combo-ticket gives you all three for €17.

Hours: Museum and treasury open daily 9:00-18:00, mid-Oct-March 10:00-17:00; theater generally open Mon-Sat 14:00-18:00, Sun from 9:00, longer hours Aug-mid-Sept; last entry one hour before closing for all three sights.

Information: +49 89 290 671, www.residenz-muenchen.de.

Getting In: The entrances on Max-Joseph-Platz and Residenzstrasse both lead to the ticket office, gift shop, and start of the treasury and Residenz Museum tours. If you run out of time or energy, you can reenter with the same ticket on another day to visit anything you missed.

Residenz vs. Nymphenburg: If you're unsure about which of Munich's top two palaces to visit, the Residenz is much more central, but Nymphenburg (□ see the Nymphenburg Tour chapter), which didn't need to be rebuilt after World War II, has the finest staterooms, a wonderful coach museum, and a vast and delight-filled park.

Starring: St. George reliquary and official royal regalia in the Treasury; the Antiquarium and the Ornate Rooms in the Residenz Museum.

The Residenz—the "residence" of Bavaria's rulers

Lions stand guard at the Residenz.

The Crown of Henry II

St. George reliquary

THE TOUR BEGINS

We'll start with the Residenz Treasury—small, manageable, and dazzling. Then we'll hike through the sprawling palace called the Residenz Museum. The Cuvilliés Theater is a quick dollop of architectural whipped cream at the end.

Residenz Treasury (Schatzkammer)

The treasury shows off a thousand years of Wittelsbach crowns and knickknacks. You'll see the regalia used in Bavaria's coronation ceremonies, the revered sacred objects that gave the Wittelsbachs divine legitimacy, and miscellaneous wonders that dazzled their European relatives. It's the best treasury in Bavaria, with fine 13th- and 14th-century crowns and delicately carved ivory and glass.

Take full advantage of the included audioguide (just punch in the number for whichever treasures catch your eye for the commentary) to make this one of the historic and artistic highlights of the city.

Room 1: The oldest jewels are 200 years older than Munich itself. Treasures of particular interest line the left wall. The gem-studded Crown of Kunigunde is associated with the saintly Bavarian queen who was crowned Holy Roman Empress in 1014 by the pope in St. Peter's Basilica in Rome. The pearl-studded prayer book of Charles the Bald (Charlemagne's grandson) allowed the book's owner to claim royal roots dating all the way back to that first Holy Roman Emperor crowned in 800. The spiky Crown of an English Queen (a.k.a. the Palatine Crown, c. 1370) is actually England's oldest crown, brought to Munich by an English princess who married a Wittelsbach duke. In the last case, the angel-and-gilt-embellished Crown of Henry II (c.

1270-1280) dates from Munich's roots, when the town was emerging as a regional capital.

Along the right side of the room are religious objects such as reliquaries and portable altars. The tiny mobile altar allowed a Carolingian king (from Charlemagne's family of kings) to pack light in 890—and still have a little Mass while on the road. Many of the precious and very old objects in this room came from various prince-bishops' collections when they were secularized (and their realms came under Bavarian rule in the Napoleonic era, c. 1800).

Room 3: Study the reliquary with St. George killing the dragon—sparkling with more than 2,000 precious stones. Get up close (it's OK to walk around the rope posts)...you can almost hear the dragon hissing. A gold-armored St. George, seated atop a ruby-studded ivory horse, tramples an emerald-green dragon. The golden box below contained the supposed relics of St. George, who was the patron saint of the Wittelsbachs. If you could lift the minuscule visor, you'd see that the carved ivory face of St. George is actually the Wittelsbach Duke Wilhelm V—the great champion of the Catholic Counter-Reformation—slaying the dragon of Protestantism.

Room 4: The incredibly realistic carved ivory crucifixes from 1630 were done by local artist Georg Petel, who was inspired by his friend Peter Paul Rubens' painting (now in the Alte Pinakothek). Look at the flesh of Jesus' wrist pulling around the nails. In the center of the room is the intricate portable altarpiece (1573-1574) of Duke Albrecht V, the Wittelsbach ruler who (as we'll see in the Residenz Museum) made a big mark on the Residenz.

Room 5: The freestanding glass case (#245) holds the impressive royal regalia of the 19th-century Wittelsbach kings—the crown, scepter, orb, and sword that were given to the king during the coronation ceremony. (The smaller pearl crown was for the queen.) They date from the early 1800s, when Bavaria had been conquered by Napoleon. The Wittelsbachs struck a deal that allowed them to stay in power, under the elevated title of "king" (not just "duke" or "prince-elector" or "prince-archbishop"). These objects were made in France by the same craftsmen who created Napoleon's crown. For the next century-plus, Wittelsbach kings (including Ludwig II) received these tokens of power. However, during the coronation ceremony, the crown you see was not actually placed on the king's head. It was brought in on a cushion (as it's displayed) and laid at the new monarch's feet.

Rooms 6-10: The rest of the treasury has objects that are more beautiful than historic. Admire the dinnerware made of rock crystal (Room 6), stone (Room 7), and gold and enamel (Room 8). Room 9 has a silver-gilt-and-marble replica of Trajan's Column. Finally, explore the "Exotica" of Room 10, including an ancient green Olmec figure encased in a Baroque niche and a Chinese rhino-horn bowl with a teeny-tiny Neptune inside.

▶ *After the micro-detail of the treasury, it's time to visit the expansive Residenz Museum. Stop by the audioguide desk to have your wand reprogrammed for the museum, cross the hall, and enter the...*

Residenz Museum (Residenzmuseum)

Though it's called a "museum," what's really on display here are the 90 rooms of the Residenz itself: the palace's banquet and reception halls, a couple of chapels, lots of paintings and porcelain, and the Wittelsbachs' lavish private apartments. While they did a valiant job of redecorating the rooms with period (but generally not original) furniture—chandeliers, canopied beds, Louis XIV-style chairs, old clocks, tapestries, and dinnerware of porcelain and silver—it feels like a place that was destroyed in a war and then rebuilt and gilded. But even without the patina of age, it's still a good place to glimpse the opulent lifestyle of Bavaria's late, great royal family.

(The Wittelsbachs are still around, but they're no longer royalty, so most of them have real jobs now. You may well have just passed one on the street—or shopping at Dallmayr.)

The place is big. Your visit is basically a long, one-way, follow-the-arrows hike through a massive old palace on two floors. Each room has a very brief description in English posted. The audioguide describes individual items and works of art throughout.

As you follow the arrows, at one point you'll likely be given the "long route" and "short route" options. The long route gives you a dozen or so additional apartments (not much different from what you'll have already seen). Here's brief coverage of the highlights, in the likely order of your visit.

Shell Grotto: This artificial grotto is made of volcanic tuff and covered completely in Bavarian freshwater shells. In its day, it was an exercise in man controlling nature—a celebration of the Renaissance humanism that flourished in the 1550s. Mercury—the pre-Christian god of trade and business—oversees the action. Check out the statue in the courtyard. In the Wittelsbachs' heyday, red wine would have flowed from the mermaid's breasts and dripped from Medusa's severed head.

The grotto courtyard is just one of 10 such courtyards in the complex. Like the rest of the palace, this courtyard and its grotto were destroyed by Allied bombs. After World War II, Germans had no money to contribute to the reconstruction, but they could gather shells; all the shells you see here were donated by small-town Bavarians. The grotto was rebuilt using Nazi photos as a guide.

Antiquarium: This long, low, arched hall stretches 220 feet end to end. It's the oldest room in the Residenz, built around 1550. The room was, and still is, a festival banquet hall. The ruler presided from the dais at the near end (warmed by the fireplace). Two hundred dignitaries can dine here, surrounded by allegories of the goodness of just rule on the ceiling.

The hall is lined with busts of Roman emperors. In the mid-16th century, Europe's royal families (such as the Wittelsbachs) collected and displayed such busts, implying a connection between themselves and the enlightened ancient Roman rulers. There was such huge demand for these classical statues in the courts of Europe that many of the "ancient busts" were fakes cranked out by crooked Romans. Still, a third of the statuary you see here is original.

The small paintings around the room (which survived WWII bombs because they were painted in arches) show 120 Bavarian

An artificial grotto made of shells

The Antiquarium, the palace's banquet hall

villages as they looked in 1550. Even today, when Bavarian historians want a record of how their village once looked, they come here.

Upper-Floor Apartments: Royal marriages were generally "arranged," and as these bluebloods typically led their own private lives (with no need to be monogamous), the men and women had a royal tradition of separate living quarters. Consequently, you'll walk through several different strings of "royal apartments."

You'll see lots of elegance...and lots of the Residenz Museum's forte: chandeliered rooms decorated with ceiling paintings, stucco work, tapestries, parquet floors, and period furniture. Because the bombs destroyed the roofs, and firefighters and rain ruined what survived, most ceilings—once ornately painted—are now just white.

Glance down into the All Saints' Chapel. This early-19th-century chapel, commissioned by Ludwig I, sustained severe damage in World War II, finally reopened in 2003, and now hosts popular concerts in the evening.

Court Chapel: Dedicated to Mary, this late-Renaissance/early-Baroque gem was the site of "Mad" King Ludwig's funeral after his mysterious murder—or suicide—in 1886. Though Ludwig II was not popular in political circles, he was beloved by his people, and his funeral drew huge crowds. About 75 years earlier, in 1810, his grandfather and namesake (Ludwig I) was married here. After the wedding ceremony, carriages rolled his guests to a rollicking reception, which turned out to be such a hit that it became an annual tradition—Oktoberfest.

Don't miss the **Private Chapel of Maximilian I** (Room 98), one of the most precious rooms in the palace. The miniature pipe organ (from about 1600) still works. The room is sumptuous, from the gold leaf ceiling and the fine altar with silver reliefs to the miniature dome and the walls made of scagliola (fake marble), a special mix of stucco, applied and polished. Designers liked it because it was less expensive than real marble and the color could be controlled.

Ornate Rooms (Rooms 55-62): As the name implies, these are some of the richest rooms in the palace. The Wittelsbachs were always trying to keep up with the Habsburgs, and this long string of ceremonial rooms—used for official business—was designed to impress. The decor and furniture are over-the-top Rococo. The family's art collection—which once decorated these walls—now makes up the core of the

Alte Pinakothek (you may see minor originals or copies of the famous masterpieces here).

The rooms were designed in the 1730s by François de Cuvilliés. The Belgian-born Cuvilliés first attracted notice as the clever court dwarf for the Bavarian ruler. He was sent to Paris to study art and returned to become the court architect. Besides the Residenz, he went on to also design the Cuvilliés Theater and Amalienburg at Nymphenburg Palace. Cuvilliés' style, featuring incredibly intricate stucco tracery twisted into unusual shapes, defined Bavarian Rococo. As you glide through this section of the palace, be sure to appreciate the gilded stucco ceilings above you.

The **Green Gallery** (Room 58)—named for its green silk damask wallpaper—was the ballroom. Imagine the parties they had here—aristocrats in powdered wigs, a string quartet playing Baroque tunes, a card game going on, while everyone admired the paintings on the walls or themselves reflected in the mirrors. The **State Bedroom** (Room 60), though furnished with a canopy bed, wasn't an actual bedroom—it was just for show. Rulers invited their subjects to come at morning and evening to stand at the railing and watch their boss

The Residenz is packed with elaborately stuccoed, mirrored, and chandeliered rooms.

ceremonially rise from his slumber to symbolically start and end the working day.

Perhaps the most ornate of these Ornate Rooms is the **Cabinet of Mirrors** (Room 61) and the adjoining Cabinet of Miniatures (Room 62) from 1740. In the **Cabinet of Mirrors,** notice the fun visual effects of the mirrors around you—the corner mirrors make things go on forever. Then peek inside the coral red room and imagine visiting the duke and having him take you here to ogle miniature copies of the most famous paintings of the day, composed with one-haired brushes.

You can't get out of the palace without seeing lots of Porcelain china. In the 18th century the Wittelsbachs, like many royal families, bolstered their status with an in-house porcelain works: Nymphenburg porcelain. (The family, while no longer in politics, owns the factory to this day.) See how the mirrors enhance the porcelain vases, creating the effect of infinite pedestals.

Ancestral Gallery (*Ahnengalerie,* Room 4): This was built in the 1740s to display portraits of the Wittelsbachs. All official guests had to pass through here to meet the duke (and his 100 Wittelsbach relatives). Midway down the hall, find the family tree. The tree is shown being planted by Hercules, to boost the family's royal street cred. Opposite the tree are two notable portraits: Charlemagne, the first Holy Roman Emperor, and to his right, Louis IV (wearing the same crown), the first Wittelsbach H.R.E., crowned in 1328.

Also on the ground floor are the **Halls of the Nibelungen** (*Nibelungensäle, Rooms 74-79*), which feature mythological scenes that were the basis of German composer Richard Wagner's opera *Der Ring des Nibelungen.* Wagner and "Mad" King Ludwig were friends and spent time hanging out here (c. 1864). The images in this hall could well have inspired Wagner to write his *Ring* and Ludwig to build his "fairy-tale castle," Neuschwanstein.

▶ *Your Residenz Museum tour is over. The doorway at the end of the hall leads back to the museum entrance. To visit the Cuvilliés Theater, exit the museum, return to Residenzstrasse, and take two rights. You'll enter the Chapel Courtyard by passing between the green lions standing guard. At the end of the lane (past the arch, before the fountain, on the left) you'll see the nondescript Cuvilliés sign.*

Cuvilliés Theater

In 1751, this was Germany's ultimate Rococo theater. Mozart conducted here several times.

Your visit consists of just one small-but-plush theater hall. It's an intimate, horseshoe-shaped performance venue, seating fewer than 400. The four tiers of box seats were for the four classes of society: city burghers on bottom, royalty next up (in the most elaborate seats), and lesser courtiers in the two highest tiers. The ruler occupied the large Royal Box directly opposite the stage (i.e., over the entrance doorway). "Mad" King Ludwig II occasionally bought out the entire theater to watch performances here by himself.

François Cuvilliés' interior is exquisite. Red, white, and gold hues dominate. Most of the decoration is painted wood, even parts that look like marble. Even the proscenium above the stage—seemingly draped with a red-velvet "curtain"—is actually made of carved wood. Also above the stage is an elaborate Wittelsbach coat of arms. The balconies seem to be supported by statues of the four seasons and are adorned with gold garlands. Cuvilliés achieved the Rococo ideal of giving theatergoers a multimedia experience—uniting the beauty of his creation with the beautiful performance on stage. It's still a working theater.

WWII bombs completely obliterated the old Cuvilliés Theater, which originally stood at a different location a short distance from here. Fortunately, much of the carved wooden interior had been removed from the walls and stored away for safekeeping. After the war, this entirely new building was constructed near the ruins of the old theater and paneled with the original decor. It's so heavily restored, you can almost smell the paint.

Appreciate the gilded stucco decor.

The intimate Cuvilliés Theater

Museum Quarter
Art Museums
Kunstareal (Art District)

Munich's cluster of fine museums displays art spanning from 3000 BC to the present: the Egyptian Museum, Glyptothek, Alte Pinakothek, Neue Pinakothek (currently closed for renovation), Lenbachhaus, Pinakothek der Moderne, and Museum Brandhorst.

Most people don't come to Munich for the art, but this group of museums makes a case for the city's world-class status. The Alte Pinakothek is the best of the bunch, with classic paintings by Da Vinci, Raphael, Dürer, Rubens, and Rembrandt, but modern art is also surprisingly well represented.

ORIENTATION

Planning Your Time: The average mortal should probably see no more than two or three museums in a single three-hour visit. Art superheroes might be able to refresh in a classy museum café, then manage one or two more.

Day Pass: A €12 day pass covers the Pinakotheks, plus the Brandhorst and Schack Collection (more 19th-century German Romanticism), on a single day. On Sundays, these museums let you in for €1 but charge €5 for the useful audioguides (normally included).

Getting There: The neighborhood is just a brisk 10-minute walk from the old center and from the train station. The Glyptothek and Lenbachhaus are near the Königsplatz stop on the U-2 subway line. The three Pinakothek museums, the Egyptian Museum, and the Brandhorst are a few blocks to the northeast. From Karlsplatz (between the train station and Marienplatz), tram #27 whisks you right to the Pinakothek and Karolinenplatz stops. You can also take bus #100 from the train station to any of the museums.

Alte Pinakothek: €7; Tue 10:00-20:30, Wed-Sun until 18:00, closed Mon; Barer Strasse 27, +49 89 2380 5216, www.pinakothek.de/alte-pinakothek.

Neue Pinakothek: Closed for renovation through 2025; museum's highlights on display at the Alte Pinakothek (+49 89 2380 5195, www.pinakothek.de/neue-pinakothek).

Pinakothek der Moderne: €10; Tue-Sun 10:00-18:00, Thu until 20:00, closed Mon; Barer Strasse 40, +49 89 2380 5360, www.pinakothek.de/pinakothek-der-moderne.

Egyptian Museum: €7; Tue 10:00-20:00, Wed-Sun until 18:00, closed Mon; Gabelsbergerstrasse 35—enter at corner of Arcisstrasse and look for the stairs leading down, +49 89 2892 7630, www.smaek.de.

Lenbachhaus: €10, includes well-done audioguide; ticket gets you half-price admission to Jewish History Museum and Munich City Museum (or use either of those tickets to get half-price admission here); Tue-Sun 10:00-18:00, Thu until 20:00, closed Mon; Luisentrasse 33, +49 89 2339 6933, www.lenbachhaus.de.

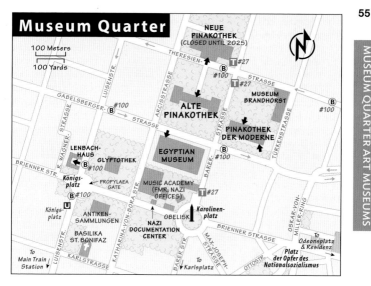

TOURING THE MUSEUMS

▲▲Alte Pinakothek

The Alte Pinakothek ("Old Art Gallery") is truly one of Europe's great collections of paintings. It shows off European masterpieces from the 14th to 19th century, starring the two tumultuous centuries (1450-1650) when Europe went from medieval to modern. See paintings from the Italian Renaissance (Raphael, Leonardo, Botticelli, Titian) and the German Renaissance it inspired (Albrecht Dürer). The Reformation of Martin Luther split Europe into two subcultures—Protestant and Catholic—with two distinct art styles (exemplified by Rembrandt and Rubens, respectively).

While the Neue Pinakothek across the street is closed, the greatest hits of its collection (1800-1920, including Impressionists and Van Gogh) are in a special ground floor exhibit at the Alte Pinakothek (included in your ticket).

▶ *The paintings we'll see are all on the upper floor, which is laid out like a barbell. Start at one fat end and work your way through the "handle"* to the other end. *From the ticket counter, head up the stairway to the left to reach the first rooms.*

German Renaissance (Room II): Albrecht Altdorfer's *The Battle of Issus (Schlacht bei Issus)* shows a world at war. Masses of soldiers are swept along in the currents and tides of a battle completely beyond their control, their confused motion reflected in the swirling sky. We see the battle from a great height, giving us a godlike perspective. Though the painting depicts Alexander the Great's history-changing victory over the Persians (find the Persian king Darius turning and fleeing), it could as easily have been Germany in the 1520s. Christians were fighting Muslims, peasants battled masters, and Catholics and Protestants were squaring off for a century of conflict. The armies melt into a huge landscape, leaving the impression that the battle goes on forever.

Albrecht Dürer's *Self-Portrait in Fur Coat (Selbstbildnis im Pelzrock)* looks like Jesus Christ but is actually 28-year-old Dürer himself (per his inscription: "XXVIII"), gazing out, with his right hand solemnly giving a blessing. This is the ultimate image of humanism: the artist as an instrument of God's continued creation. Get close and enjoy the intricately braided hair, the skin texture, and the fur collar. To the left of the head is Dürer's famous monogram—"A.D." in the form of a pyramid.

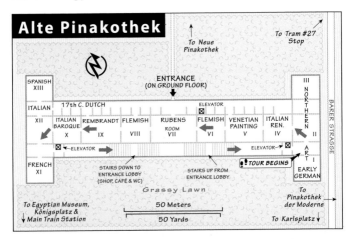

Altdorfer shows a world at war.

Dürer's self-portrait—artist as saint

Italian Renaissance (Room IV): With the Italian Renaissance—the "rebirth" of interest in the art and learning of ancient Greece and Rome—artists captured the realism, three-dimensionality, and symmetry found in classical statues. Twenty-one-year-old Leonardo da Vinci's *Virgin and Child (Maria mit dem Kinde)* need no halos—they radiate purity. Mary is a solid pyramid of maternal love, flanked by Renaissance-arch windows that look out on the hazy distance. Baby Jesus reaches out to play innocently with a carnation, the blood-colored symbol of his eventual death.

Raphael's *Holy Family at the Canigiani House (Die hl. Familie aus dem Hause Canigiani)* takes Leonardo's pyramid form and runs with it. Father Joseph forms the peak, with his staff as the strong central axis. Mary and Jesus (on the right) form a pyramid-within-the-pyramid, as do Elizabeth and baby John the Baptist on the left. They all exchange meaningful eye contact, safe within the bounds of the stable family structure.

In Botticelli's *Lamentation over Christ (Die Beweinung Christi)*, the Renaissance "pyramid" implodes, as the weight of the dead Christ drags everyone down, and the tomb grins darkly behind them.

This early Da Vinci has his trademark pyramid composition and fantasy landscape.

Venetian Painting (Room V): In Titian's *Christ Crowned with Thorns (Die Dornenkrönung),* a powerfully built Christ sits silently enduring torture by prison guards. The painting is by Venice's greatest Renaissance painter, but there's no symmetry, no pyramid form, and the brushwork is intentionally messy and Impressionistic. By the way, this is the first painting we've seen done on canvas rather than wood, as artists experimented with vegetable oil-based paints.

Rubens and Baroque (Room VII): Europe's religious wars split the Continent in two—Protestants in the northern countries, Catholics in the south. (Germany itself was divided, with Bavaria remaining Catholic.) The Baroque style, popular in Catholic countries, featured large canvases, bright colors, lots of flesh, rippling motion, wild emotions, grand themes...and pudgy winged babies, the sure sign of Baroque. This room holds several canvases by the great Flemish painter Peter Paul Rubens.

In Rubens' 300-square-foot *Great Last Judgment (Das Grosse Jüngste Gericht),* Christ raises the righteous up to heaven (left side) and damns the sinners to hell (on the right). This swirling cycle of nudes was considered risqué and kept under wraps by the very monks who'd commissioned it.

Titian signals the end of the Renaissance.　　　Rubens and his first wife, Isabella

Rubens and Isabella Brant in the Honeysuckle Bower shows the artist with his first wife, both of them the very picture of health, wealth, and success. They lean together unconsciously, as people in love will do, with their hands clasped in mutual affection. When his first wife died, 53-year-old Rubens found a replacement—16-year-old Hélène Fourment, shown in an adjacent painting (just to the left) in her wedding dress. You may recognize Hélène's face in other Rubens paintings.

The *Rape of the Daughters of Leucippus (Der Raub der Töchter des Leukippos)* has many of Rubens' most typical elements—fleshy, emotional, rippling motion; bright colors; and a classical subject. The legendary twins Castor and Pollux crash a wedding and steal the brides as their own. The chaos of flailing limbs and rearing horses is all held together in a subtle X-shaped composition. Like the weaving counterpoint in a Baroque fugue, Rubens balances opposites.

Notice that Rubens' canvases were—to a great extent—cranked out by his students and assistants from small "cartoons" the master himself made (displayed in the side room).

Rembrandt and Dutch (Room IX): Rembrandt van Rijn's *Six Paintings from the Life of Christ* are a down-to-earth look at

Rubens specialized in tourist-dwarfing canvases populated with nudes in complex compositions.

supernatural events. *The Holy Family (Die Heilige Familie)* is set in a carpenter's workshop (with tools on the wall). The canvases are dark brown, lit by strong light. The *Holy Family*'s light source is the Baby Jesus himself—literally the "light of the world." In the *Raising of the Cross (Kreuzaufrichtung)*, a man dressed in blue is looking on—a self-portrait of Rembrandt.

In the *Deposition (Kreuzabnahme)*, the light bounces off Christ's pale body onto his mother Mary, who has fainted in the shadows, showing how his death also hurts her. The drama is underplayed, with subdued emotions.

▲Neue Pinakothek

The Neue Pinakothek's easy-to-like collection of paintings from 1800 to 1920 includes world-class Impressionist paintings and one of Van Gogh's *Sunflowers*. The building is closed for renovations through 2025; in the meantime, highlights from its collection are on display at the Alte Pinakothek.

▲Pinakothek der Moderne

This museum picks up where the other two Pinakotheks leave off, covering the 20th and 21st centuries. The museum's impressive permanent collection is shown according to various themes that come and go a couple of times a year, rather than in periods or by artist. These rotating displays are supplemented by often worthwhile temporary exhibits. The design wing, in the basement, is also worth a quick look. From chairs to bikes to blenders to cars and computers, these are everyday objects that work efficiently but also have a sleek artistic flair. It's free to step into the atrium of the striking, white, high-ceilinged building.

▲▲Lenbachhaus

Munich blew the art world's mind when a bunch of art-school cronies formed the revolutionary "Blue Rider" (Blauer Reiter) group and galloped toward a brand-new horizon—abstract art. In the pleasant galleries at the Lenbachhaus, you can witness the birth of Modernist nonrepresentational art, then stroll the rest of the building's offerings (including the apartments of painter Franz von Lenbach, whose original villa and studio are now largely enclosed by the modern museum building).

The Pinakothek der Moderne has Kandinsky... ...as does the underrated Lenbachhaus.

▶ *The Blue Rider movement begins on the second floor, with seemingly innocuous paintings of the cute Bavarian town of Murnau.*

Origins of the Blue Rider Group: It was here in 1908 that two Munich couples—Wassily Kandinsky and Gabriele Münter, and Alexej Jawlensky and Marianne von Werefkin—came for vacation. The four painted together—it's hard to tell their work apart—employing intense colors, thick paint, and bold black outlines. Over the next few years (c. 1911-1914), they gathered into a group of Munich-based artists calling themselves the Blue Rider, which included Paul Klee and Franz Marc. They were all devoted to expressing the spiritual truths they felt within by using intense colors and geometric shapes.

The Blue Rider School was blown apart by World War I. The artists who survived the Great War went on to pioneer abstract art. Over time, they paid less attention to re-creating the physical world realistically on canvas and more attention to the colors and lines alone. Russian expat Kandinsky's "Improvisations"—like a jazz musician improvising a new pattern of notes from a set scale—eventually became the art world's first purely abstract canvases. Soon Kandinsky was teaching at the famous Bauhaus school in Weimar, and his style spread everywhere. Jawlensky and Klee also went on to develop a simpler and more abstract style. Such artists infuriated Hitler, who termed their work "degenerate."

First Floor: This floor has temporary exhibitions, as well as two permanent sections. One displays several oddball installations by 20th-century German artist Joseph Beuys. (Is that art, or did the janitor just leave a broom here?) The other, in the far wing, is a stash of

19th-century paintings that provides a nice contrast to all the abstract stuff.

Ground Floor: Next to the ticket desk, walk into the mustard-colored villa of Franz von Lenbach himself (encapsulated within the museum building). Of modest means and from a small town, Lenbach turned his childhood passion for painting into a successful career, executing portraits of 19th-century notables and doing well enough to build this lavish home (sold to the city by his widow in the 1920s). Head up the stairs, where four ornate rooms, with views over the garden, have been preserved; Lenbach's own paintings cover the walls.

More Museums

To enjoy the ▲ **Egyptian Museum** you don't need a strong interest in ancient Egypt. With its smart design and touch-screen terminals, you feel like you're deep in an ancient tomb with beautifully lit art. The **Museum Brandhorst** covers late-20th-century/early-21st-century art (Andy Warhol, Cy Twombly), contained in a colorful building (closed Mon). The **Glyptothek** is an impressive collection of Greek and Roman sculpture (closed Mon). The **Nazi Documentation Center** is also in this quarter—for details see page 86.

Nymphenburg Palace Tour

For 200 years, this royal retreat of palaces and gardens was the Wittelsbach rulers' summer vacation home, a getaway from the sniping politics of court life in the city. Their kids frolicked in the ponds and gardens, while the adults played cards, listened to music, and sipped coffee on the veranda.

Today, Nymphenburg Palace and the surrounding one-square-mile park are a great place for a royal stroll or discreet picnic. Indoors, you can tour the Bavarian royal family's summer quarters, visit the Royal Stables Museum (carriages, sleighs, and porcelain), and browse a few mini-palaces on the grounds. Allow at least three hours (including travel time) to see the palace complex at a leisurely pace.

ORIENTATION

Cost: €8 for the palace; €6 for the Royal Stables Museum; €15 combo-ticket (€12 off-season) covers the palace, Royal Stables Museum, and outlying sights.

Hours: All sights open daily 9:00-18:00, mid-Oct-March 10:00-16:00—except for Amalienburg and the other small palaces in the park, which close in winter; park open daily 6:00-dusk and free to enter.

Information: +49 89 179 080, www.schloss-nymphenburg.de.

Getting There: The palace is three miles northwest of central Munich. Take tram #17 (direction: Amalienburgstrasse) from the train station or Karlsplatz. In 15 minutes you reach the Schloss Nymphenburg stop. From the bridge by the tram stop, you'll see the palace—a 10-minute walk away. The palace is a pleasant 30-minute bike ride from the main train station, following Nymphenburger Strasse. Biking is not permitted within the palace grounds.

Tours: An audioguide for Nymphenburg Palace is available for €3.50.

Eating: A café serves lunch and snacks in a winter garden or on a nice terrace, a five-minute walk behind and to the right of the palace (open year-round). More eating options are near the Schloss Nymphenburg tram stop.

THE TOUR BEGINS

Nymphenburg Palace

In 1662, after 10 years of trying, the Bavarian ruler Ferdinand Maria

Grand entrance to Nymphenburg Palace

Ludwig I and his ladies

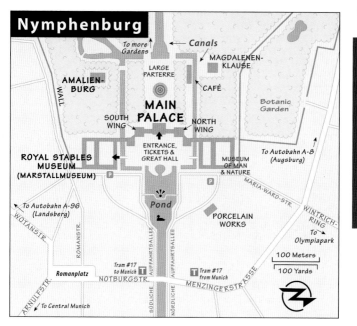

and his wife, Henriette Adelaide of Savoy, finally had a son, Max Emanuel. In gratitude for a male heir, Ferdinand gave this land to his Italian wife, who proceeded to build an Italian-style Baroque palace as their summer residence. Their son expanded the palace to its current size. (Today's Wittelsbachs, who still refer to themselves as "princes" or "dukes," live in one wing of the palace.)

▶ *Start your visit in the Schlossgeschichte (palace history) room at the entry for a good intro. Then make your way to the...*

Great Hall (a.k.a. Stone Hall)

As the central room of the palace, this light and airy space was the dining hall, site of big Wittelsbach family festivals. One of the grandest and best-preserved Rococo rooms in Bavaria (from about 1760), it sports elaborate stucco work and a ceiling fresco by Johann Baptist Zimmermann (of Wieskirche fame).

The Great Hall has views of nature out the windows and in the painted scenes on the ceiling.

Zimmermann's fresco opens a sunroof to the heavens, where Greek gods cavort. In the sunny center, Apollo drives his chariot to bring the dawn, while bearded Zeus (astride an eagle) and peacock-carrying Juno look on. The rainbow symbolizes the peace brought by the enlightened Wittelsbachs. Around the borders of the painting, notice the fun optical illusions: For example, a painted dog holds a stucco bird in its mouth. The painting's natural setting and joie de vivre reflect the pastoral pleasures enjoyed here. And at one end of the fresco (away from the windows) lounges a lovely maiden with flowers in her hair: It's Flora, the eponymous nymph who inspired this "nymph's castle"—Nymphenburg.

From here, two wings stretch to the left and right. They're mirror images of one another: antechamber, audience chamber, bedchamber, and private living quarters. Guests would arrive here in the Great Hall for an awe-inspiring first impression, then make their way through a series of (also impressive) waiting rooms for their date with the Wittelsbach nobility.

▶ The tour continues in the...

North Wing (Rooms 2-9)

Breeze quickly through this less interesting wing, filled with tapestries and Wittelsbach portraits (including curly-haired Max Emanuel, who built this wing). Pause in the long corridor **(the North Gallery)** lined with paintings of various Wittelsbach palaces. The names of each are labeled on gilded plaques. The ones of Nymphenburg show the place around 1720, back when there was nothing but countryside between it and downtown (and gondolas plied the canals). Find the painting of Fürstenried Palace (in another Munich suburb) and look for the twin onion domes of the Frauenkirche in the distance. Of the countless paintings you'll see, many depict palaces the family owned throughout their realm...just showing off.

▶ *Return to the Great Hall and enter the other wing.*

South Wing (Rooms 10-20)

Pass through the gold-and-white Room 10 and turn right into the red-walled **South Apartment Antechamber.** The room calls up the exuberant time of Nymphenburg's founding couple, Ferdinand and Henriette. A portrait on the wall shows them posing together in their rich courtly dress. The large painting on the left depicts the family in a Greek myth: Henriette (as the moon goddess) leads her youngest son Joseph Clemens by the hand, while her first son Max Emanuel (as Hercules) receives the gift of a sword. On the right side of the room, Ferdinand is represented as Endymion, a mortal loved by the moon goddess. The ceiling painting (of the earth goddess Cybele) also dates from the time of Nymphenburg's first family.

▶ *After admiring the Queen's Bedroom and Chinese lacquer cabinet, head back down the long hall to...*

King Ludwig I's Gallery of Beauties

The room is decorated top to bottom with portraits of 36 beautiful women (all painted by Joseph Stieler between 1826 and 1850). Ludwig I was a consummate girl-watcher.

Ludwig prided himself on his ability to appreciate beauty regardless of social rank. He enjoyed picking out the prettiest women from the general public and, with one of the most effective pickup lines of all time, inviting them to the palace for a portrait. Who could refuse? The portraits were on public display in the Residenz and catapulted their subjects to stardom. The women range from commoners to princesses, but notice that they share one physical trait: Ludwig obviously preferred brunettes. The portraits are done in the modest and slightly sentimental Biedermeier style popular in central Europe, as opposed to the more flamboyant Romanticism (so beloved of Ludwig's "mad" grandson) also in vogue at that time.

Most of these portraits have rich stories behind them (each of the following is at eye level): Find Helene Sedlmayr, a humble cobbler's daughter who caught Ludwig's eye; she poses in a blue-and-gray dress way beyond her budget. Though poor, she was considered Munich's comeliest *Fräulein,* and she eventually married the king's valet and had 10 children. Lady Jane Ellenborough—an elegant English baroness— went through four marriages and numerous affairs, including one with Ludwig (and, much later, with his son Otto, after Otto had become king of Greece). She was fluent in nine languages, including Arabic, after marrying a Syrian sheik 20 years her junior.

Lola Montez was the king's most notorious mistress, who led him to his downfall. The portrait shows her the year she met Ludwig (she was 29, he was 60), wearing the black-lace mantilla and red flowers of a Spanish dancer. This Irish beauty (born Maria Gilbert) eventually made her way to Munich. Ludwig was so bedazzled that he gave her a title—Countess of Landsfeld—along with a hefty annual income. Near Lola, the woman half-cloaked in a red-and-ermine robe is Princess Marie of Prussia—Ludwig's daughter-in-law—who once lived in the

Commoner Helene Sedlmayr caught Ludwig's eye.

Lady Jane Ellenborough, a Ludwig mistress

last rooms we'll visit. (And where in the Gallery of Beauties is the portrait of Ludwig's wife, Queen Therese? She's not here...you'll have to duck into the elegant, green Queen's Study to see her portrait.)

▸ *Pass through the blue Audience Room (with elaborate curtain rods and mahogany furniture in the French-inspired Empire style—what we'd call Neoclassical) and into the (other)...*

Queen's Bedroom

The room has much the same furniture it had on August 25, 1845, when Princess Marie gave birth to the future King Ludwig II. Little Ludwig (see his bust, next to brother Otto's) was greatly inspired by Nymphenburg—riding horses in summer, taking sleigh rides in winter, reading poetry at Amalienburg. The love of nature and solitude he absorbed at Nymphenburg eventually led Ludwig to abandon Munich for his castles in the remote Bavarian countryside. By the way, note the mirror in this bedroom. Royal births were carefully witnessed, and the mirror allowed for a better view. While Ludwig's birth was well documented, his death was shrouded in mystery (see page 130).

▸ *When you're ready to leave the palace, there's much more to see on the grounds and in the outlying buildings. First up: the Royal Stables Museum—to the left of the main palace (as you approach the complex).*

Royal Stables Museum (Marstallmuseum)

These former stables are full of gilded coaches worthy of a Cinderella dream. In the big entrance hall is a golden carriage drawn by eight white horses. In 1742, it carried Karl Albrecht Wittelsbach to Frankfurt to be crowned Holy Roman Emperor. As emperor, he got eight horses—kings got only six. The event is depicted in a frieze stretching the length of the museum wall; Karl's carriage is #159. Look closely at the carriage's ornamentation. It's pure Rococo (a term that comes from the word "shell"). Next are more royal carriages, including the carriage of the first king of Bavaria (crowned by Napoleon in 1806). Then come Wittelsbach sleighs from the 1600s.

Around the corner, it's all Ludwig II. Ludwig was a Rococo nut and commissioned work to be done in Neo-Rococo, proving that even Rococo can be outdone. Lining the wall are the king's "beauties"—his favorite horses, each with a pet name. The king poses at the end of the hall. The last rooms, starting with the 1866 portrait of Ludwig in the saddle, are a celebration of Ludwig's love of riding. Paintings show the king's horses being served almost like humans.

Upstairs is a collection of Nymphenburg porcelain, made for the royal family on the premises in their private factory (which is still in operation today but not open to the public). You'll see plates and cups painted in various styles, from ancient Greek to Old Masters, Romantic, and Art Nouveau.

Palace Grounds

The wooded grounds extend far back beyond the formal gardens and are popular with joggers and walkers. Find a bench for a low-profile picnic. The park is laced with canals and small lakes, where court guests once rode on Venetian-style gondolas. On the grounds are four small "extra" palaces buried in the park (included on the combo-ticket): Pagodenburg, a Chinese-inspired pavilion; Badenburg, an opulent bathing house and banquet hall; the Magdalenenklause, a mini palace that looks like a ruin from the outside but has an elaborate altar and woody apartments inside; and the most worthwhile, Amalienburg.

▶ *Three hundred yards from Nymphenburg Palace, head into the sculpted garden and veer to the left, following signs to reach...*

Amalienburg

In 1734, Prince-Elector Karl Albrecht had this little Rococo hunting lodge built for his wife, Maria Amalia. Amalienburg was designed by François de Cuvilliés (of Residenz fame) and decorated by Johann Baptist Zimmermann. The facade—with a pink-and-white grand entryway—is graced by an image of Diana, goddess of the chase, flanked by satyrs.

Inside, you get a sense of how the Wittelsbachs loved to hunt. Doghouses under gun cupboards fill the first room. In the fine yellow-and-silver bedroom, the bed is flanked by portraits of Karl Albrecht and Maria Amalia—decked out in hunting attire. She liked her dogs. The door under her portrait leads to stairs to the rooftop. From up there, the queen would shoot pheasants stirred up by the dogs—like skeet shooting.

The mini Hall of Mirrors is a blue-and-silver commotion of Rococo nymphs designed by Cuvilliés. In the next room, paintings depict court festivities, formal hunting parties, and no-contest kills (where the animal is put at an impossible disadvantage—like shooting fish in a barrel). Finally, the sparse kitchen is decorated with Chinese-style drawings on Dutch tile.

Dachau Concentration Camp Memorial Tour

Gedenkstätte Dachau

Dachau was the first Nazi concentration camp (1933). Today, it's an easily accessible memorial for travelers and an effective voice from our recent but grisly past, pleading, "Never again."

A visit to Dachau is a powerful and valuable experience and, when approached thoughtfully, well worth the effort it takes to get here. Many visitors come away from Dachau with more respect for history and the dangers of mixing fear, the promise of jobs, blind patriotism, and an evil government. You'll likely see lots of high-school students here, as it's a frequent field-trip destination.

ORIENTATION

Cost and Hours: Free, daily 9:00-17:00. Some areas may begin to close before 17:00—plan to wrap up by 16:40 to allow time to walk back to the entrance. The museum discourages parents from bringing children under age 14.

Information: +49 8131 669 970, www.kz-gedenkstaette-dachau.de.

Planning Your Time: Allow about five hours—three hours at the camp, plus time for round-trip travel from central Munich. With limited time you could do the whole trip in as little as 3.5 hours by focusing on the museum and skipping the walk to the memorials and crematorium.

Getting There on Your Own: The camp is 45 minutes from downtown Munich. By **public transit,** take the S-2 (end station: Petershausen or Altomünster) from any of the central S-Bahn stops to Dachau (3/hour, 20-minute trip from Hauptbahnhof). Then, at Dachau station, follow the crowds out to the bus platforms. Find the sign for *KZ-Gedenkstätte/Concentration Camp Memorial Site* and catch bus #726 (6/hour, 3/hour on Sun). Ride it seven minutes to the KZ-Gedenkstätte stop. (The return bus stop is across the street.)

An M-1 public transit day ticket (*Single-Tageskarte*) covers the entire trip, both ways (see page 173).

Getting There by Guided Tour: Radius Tours offers a great value. Allow roughly five hours total. It's smart to reserve the day before, especially for morning tours (€35, RS%—select "student rate" when booking online; tours run daily year-round at 9:00, additional departures in summer, leaves from Dachauer Strasse 4 near Munich train station, +49 89 543 487 7740, www.radiustours.com).

Services: Outside the camp wall, the visitors center has a small cafeteria, sheltered benches where you can eat, a bookstore with English-language books on Holocaust themes, and a WC (more WCs inside the camp).

Tours: The €4.50 **audioguide** covers the grounds and museum but isn't essential as the camp is fully labeled in English (cash only, leave ID). Two different **guided walks** in English start from the visitors center (€4, at 11:00 and 13:00, 2.5 hours; limited to 30 people, fills fast—especially in summer).

THE TOUR BEGINS

From the visitors center, approach the main compound. You enter, like the inmates did, through the infamous **iron gate** that held the taunting slogan *Arbeit macht frei* ("Work makes you free"). The original sign was stolen in 2014 and replaced with a replica.

▶ *Step through the gate into the camp grounds. Inside are the four key experiences of the memorial: the museum (just to your right), the bunker (behind the museum), the restored barracks (to your left), and a pensive walk (heading far to your left) across the huge but now-empty camp to the memorials and crematorium at the far end. Enter the museum.*

Museum

The museum is housed in a former camp maintenance building. Just inside is a small bookshop that funds a nonprofit organization (founded by former prisoners) that researches and preserves the camp's history. Immediately to the right of the door you entered, check showtimes for the museum's powerful 40-minute documentary film

"Work makes you free"...the empty promise inmates saw as they entered Dachau

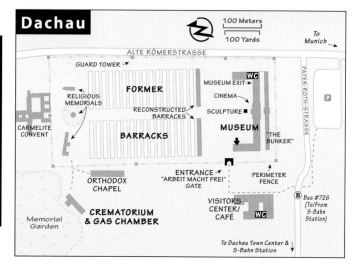

(described later). The museum is organized chronologically, everything is thoughtfully described in English, and touch screens let you watch early newsreels.

The Camp Is Founded (Rooms 1-2): On January 30, 1933, Adolf Hitler took power. Two months later, Dachau opened. It was a "concentration" camp, to gather together and isolate enemies of the state so they could not infect the rest of society. The camp was built well outside Dachau's residential zone, surrounded by a mile-wide restricted area.

A map of the Nazi camp system shows that Dachau was just one of many such camps. Some were concentration camps (marked with a square, like Dachau). Others (marked with a triangle with a V) were extermination camps—Auschwitz, Sobibor—built with the express purpose of executing people on a mass scale. Nearby, photos and posters chronicle the rise of Hitler in the 1920s: the resentment bred by Germany's defeat in World War I, the weak Weimar Republic, Hitler's solution to Germany's problems (blame the Jews), his failed Beer Hall Putsch, his participation in mainstream politics. No sooner did he take power than he suspended democracy and began squelching all opposition.

Life at the Camp (Rooms 3-7): In 1933, the first prisoners passed through the *Arbeit macht frei* gates. They were classified and labeled with a badge (see the chart in Room 4) according to their "crime" against the state. Besides political activists (communists and leftist intellectuals), prisoners included homosexuals, Jehovah's Witnesses, Roma and Sinti ("Gypsies"), so-called career criminals, "asocials," and Germans who had tried to flee the country. A special badge—the yellow Star of David—was reserved for a group the Nazis particularly loathed: Jews.

The camp was run by the SS, the organization (headed by mastermind Heinrich Himmler) charged with Germany's internal security. Dachau was a training center for future camp managers. Rudolf Höss, who worked at Dachau from 1934 to 1938, went on to become the first commandant of Auschwitz.

Life at Dachau was horrific. It was a work camp, where inmates were expected to pay for their "crimes" with slave labor. The camp was strictly regimented: a wake-up call at 4:00, an 11-hour workday, roll call at 5:15 and 19:00, lights out at 21:00. The work was hard, whether quarrying or hauling loads or constructing the very buildings you see today. The rations were meager. Rule-breakers were punished severely—all manner of torture took place here. The most common punishment was being forced to stand at attention until you collapsed.

On September 1, 1939, Germany invaded Poland, World War II began, and Dachau's role changed.

Cinema: The 40-minute film is a sobering, graphic, and sometimes grisly account of the rise of Hitler and the atrocities of the camp (usually shown in English at 10:15, 11:45, and 14:00).

The War Years (Rooms 8-15): Once the war began, conditions at

As soon as Hitler took power...

...dissidents were rounded up and labeled.

Dachau deteriorated. The original camp had been designed to hold just under 3,000 inmates. In 1937 and 1938, the camp was expanded and the building that now houses the museum was built, along with barracks intended to hold 6,000 prisoners. With the war, the prisoner population swelled, and the Nazis found other purposes for the camp. It was less a concentration camp for German dissidents and more a dumping ground for foreigners, POWs, and even 2,000 Catholic priests. From Dachau, Jewish prisoners were sent east to the gas chambers. Inmates were used as slave labor for the German war machine—many were shipped to nearby satellite camps to make armaments. Prisoners were used as human guinea pigs for war-related medical experiments of human tolerance for air pressure, hypothermia, and biological agents like malaria; the photos of these victims are especially painful to view.

As the Allies closed in on both fronts, Dachau was bursting with more than 30,000 prisoners jammed into its 34 barracks. In the winter of 1944-1945, disease broke out (including typhus and dysentery), and food ran short. Deaths in the camp increased dramatically—from 403 (October 1944) to 3,991 (February 1945). With coal for the crematorium running low, those who died were buried in mass graves outside the camp site. The Allies arrived on April 29. After 12 years of existence, Dachau was finally liberated, but more than 1,000 prisoners were so weak or sick that they died soon after.

Postscript: All told, about 40,000 people died at Dachau and its satellite camps between 1933 and 1945. (By comparison, more than a million were killed at Auschwitz in Poland.) But Dachau remains notorious because it was the Nazis' first camp. Oddly, Dachau actually housed people longer *after* the war than during the war. First, it housed Nazi officials arrested by the Allies, as they awaited trial at Nürnberg for war crimes. From 1948 to 1964, the camp became cheap housing for ethnic Germans expelled from Eastern Europe, complete with a cinema, shops, and so on. The last of the barracks was torn down in 1964, and the museum opened the following year.

▶ *Consider using the WC before leaving the museum building (there aren't any bathrooms elsewhere within the camp walls). Find the side door, at the end of the exhibition, which leads out to the long, low bunker behind the museum building.*

Prisoners at Dachau were subject to torture, such as standing at attention for long periods.

Bunker

This was a cellblock for prominent "special prisoners," such as failed Hitler assassins, German religious leaders, and politicians who challenged Nazism. Most of the 136 cells are empty, but exhibits in a few of them (near the entrance) profile the inmates and the SS guards who worked at Dachau, and allow you to listen to some inmates' testimonies. Cell #2 was the interrogation room. Cell #9 was a "standing cell"—inmates were tortured here by being forced to stay on their feet for days at a time.

▸ *Exit the bunker and walk around past the* Arbeit macht frei *gate to the big square between the museum and the reconstructed barracks, which was used for roll call. In front of the museum, notice the powerful memorial to the victims, created in 1968 by Nandor Glid, a Jewish Holocaust survivor and artist, which includes humanity's vow:* Never Again. *Cross the square to the farther of the two reconstructed...*

Barracks

Take a quick look inside to get an idea of what sleeping and living conditions were like in the camp. There were 34 barracks, each measuring about 10 yards by 100 yards. When the camp was at its fullest, there was only about one square yard of living space per inmate. The original barracks were torn down in 1962.

▸ *Now walk between the two reconstructed barracks and down the tree-lined path past the gravel beds that mark the footprints of the other barracks.*

Many prisoners were worked to death.

Others were tortured in the bunker cells.

Memorials dot the grounds, where visitors can ponder the camp and its motto: "Never Again."

Sights at the Far End of the Camp

At the end of the camp, in space that once housed the camp vegetable garden, rabbit farm, and brothel, there are now three places of meditation and worship (Jewish to your right, Catholic straight ahead, and Protestant to your left). Beyond them, just outside the camp, is a Carmelite convent.

▶ *Turn left toward the corner of the camp and find the small bridge leading (past a Russian Orthodox chapel) to the...*

Camp Crematorium

A memorial garden surrounds the two camp crematorium buildings, which were used to burn the bodies of prisoners who had died or been killed. The newer, larger concrete crematorium was built to replace the smaller wooden one. One of its rooms is a gas chamber, which worked on the same principles as the much larger one at Auschwitz, and was originally disguised as a shower room (the fittings are gone now). It was never put to use at Dachau for mass murder, but survivors have testified that small groups were killed in it "experimentally."

▶ *To return to Munich by public transit, retrace your steps to the bus stop, where bus #726 takes you back to the Dachau train station. Then catch the S-2 to downtown Munich (direction: Erding or Markt Schwaben). The ride back to Munich gives you ample time to process all you've seen and experienced on your visit.*

More Munich Sights

The best sights in Munich are those along my Munich City Walk, and the places detailed in this book's tour chapters: the 🕮 **Residenz,** the 🕮 **Museum Quarter,** 🕮 **Nymphenburg Palace,** and 🕮 **Dachau Concentration Camp Memorial.**

But don't stop there. In this chapter, I've highlighted the best of Munich's secondary sights. You can choose from rocket science to a stroll in the park, from hot cars to city history, and from a Baroque palace to the sobering Nazi Documentation Center. Thanks to the city's excellent public transportation system, even outlying sights are less than a half-hour away. Most sights in this chapter don't require a reservation, but factory tours at BMW-Welt must be booked well in advance.

NEAR MARIENPLATZ

▲Munich City Museum (Münchner Stadtmuseum)

The museum's permanent exhibit on Munich's history (called "Typically Munich!") is interesting, but it's an exhaustive and confusing maze, and there's no posted English information. Use the following mini tour for an overview, then supplement it with the audioguide and English booklet.

Start in the ticketing hall with the wooden model showing Munich today. Find the Frauenkirche, Isar River, New Town Hall, Residenz...and no skyscrapers. The city looks remarkably similar in scale to the model (in the next room) from 1570. From here, follow the one-way tour, clearly marked with signs.

Ground Floor (Medieval): An imposing gray statue of Henry the Lion introduces us to the city's 12th-century founder. The eight statues of Morris dancers (1480) became a symbol of the vibrant market town (and the tradition continued with the New Town Hall glockenspiel's dancing coopers). On the rest of the ground floor, paintings, swords, and cherubs clad in armor (these are the original statues that stood under the Virgin Mary's column on Marienplatz) capture more medieval ambience.

First Floor (1800s): The "New Munich" was created when the city was expanded beyond the old medieval walls (see the illuminated view of the city from 1761 in the "Canaletto-Blick" opposite the top of the stairs). The city was prosperous, as evidenced by the furniture and paintings on display. In the center of the room, find big paintings ("Effigies") of the century's magnificent kings—Maximilian I,

City Museum's model of Munich in 1570

Vintage glove puppets

The City Museum has some Nazi history.

The Nazi Documentation Center has more.

Maximilian II, and Ludwig I (as well as Lola Montez, Ludwig I's most famous mistress).

Second Floor (Munich 1900): As Munich approached its 700th birthday, it was becoming aware of itself as a major capital. The Münchner Kindl logo was born. It was a city of artists (Wagner operas, Lenbach portraits, Von Stuck soirées), *Jugendstil* furniture, beer, and a cosmopolitan outlook (see the "Kaiser-Panorama," the big barrel-shaped 3-D peep show of Indian and Asian peoples). Posters illustrate a Munich forte during this period: graphic design. But after World War I, Munich became a hotbed of discontent. The "revue" room shows the city's clash of ideas: communists, capitalists, Nazis, and the anarchic theater of comedian Karl Valentin and early works by playwright Bertolt Brecht. A nearby display gives some background on Munich's role as the birthplace of Nazism (much more thoroughly covered in the museum's National Socialism wing).

Third Floor: An exhibit highlights Germany's long tradition of puppetry, from rod-and-shadow puppets to glove puppets to marionettes. Fair and Oktoberfest items such as carousel animals may attract children, but beware that horror-house displays may scare the daylights out of them (and you).

Video Finish: End your visit back on the first floor with video images capturing the contemporary Munich scene—rock music, World Cup triumphs, beer gardens, and other things that are..."typically Munich."

National Socialism Wing: Your permanent-exhibit ticket includes this small but worthwhile exhibit (in a separate building across the courtyard) of photos and uniforms that takes you chronologically

Nazism in Munich

From its very beginnings, the National Socialist German Workers' Party was linked with Bavaria. It was in Munich that Hitler and other disillusioned WWI veterans first gathered to lick their wounds. The Nazi Party was founded here in 1919, and this is where Hitler staged his attempted coup (the 1923 Beer Hall Putsch). In nearby Landsberg, he was imprisoned and wrote his *Mein Kampf* manifesto.

Once in power, Hitler officially proclaimed Munich as the "Capital of the Movement." In 1933, the Nazi government opened its first concentration camp, outside Munich in Dachau. Munich was also the site of the infamous failed peace pact, the Munich Agreement of 1938, where Britain's prime minister tried to avoid war by appeasing Hitler.

through the Nazi years, focused on Munich, from post-WWI struggles to postwar reconstruction.

▶ *€4 includes good audioguide, €7 includes temporary exhibits; ticket gets you half-price admission to Jewish History Museum, Lenbachhaus, or Villa Stuck—or use any of those tickets to get half-price admission here; open Tue-Sun 10:00-18:00, closed Mon; St.-Jakobs-Platz 1, +49 89 2332 2370, www.muenchner-stadtmuseum.de.*

In the Museum Quarter

▲▲Nazi Documentation Center
(NS-Dokumentationszentrum München)

This center documents the rise and fall of Nazism with a focus on Munich's role and the reasons behind it. While there are no actual artifacts here, the experience is moving and a worthwhile companion to visiting the Dachau Concentration Camp Memorial.

Begin on the top floor (1918-1933), which covers the end of World War I and the beginning of Hitler's movement in Munich. The third floor (1933-1939) documents the establishment of the "racially pure" Volksgemeinschaft ("people's community") and the effect of Nazi domination on everyday life. The first floor (after 1945) examines the faith people put in the Nazi regime.

In the basement, the Learning Center encourages reflection, with a library where you can delve into topics of interest, and a collection of books banned during Nazi rule. Touch-screen computer terminals let you sit and page through the center's exhibits in full.

▶ *Free, includes audioguide; Tue-Sun 10:00-19:00, closed Mon; U-2: Königsplatz, tram #27, or bus #100; along Brienner Strasse near the corner of Arcisstrasse at Max-Mannheimer-Platz 1, +49 89 2336 7000, www.ns-dokuzentrum-muenchen.de.*

Near the River

▲English Garden (Englischer Garten)

Munich's "Central Park" is the largest urban park on the Continent (established 1789). It stretches north for three miles—a vast expanse of parkland and trails dotted with beer gardens and naked sunbathers. Thousands of locals commune with nature here on sunny summer days. It's great for a walk, or—better yet—a bike ride (unfortunately, there are no bike rental outfits in or near the park; see page 175 for bike-rental places).

For the best quick visit, take bus #100 or tram #16 to the Nationalmuseum/Haus der Kunst stop. Under the bridge, you'll see surfers. (The surf's always up here—even through the night; surfers bring their own lights.) Follow the path, to the right of the surfing spot, downstream until you reach the big lawn. The Chinese Tower beer garden is just beyond the tree-covered hill to the right. Follow the oompah music and walk to the hilltop pagoda, with a postcard view of the city on your way. Afterward, instead of retracing your steps, you can walk (or take bus #54 a couple of stops) to the Giselastrasse U-Bahn station and return to town on the U-3 or U-6.

Nearby: Villa Stuck, the former home of Munich's top Art Nouveau artist (www.villastuck.de), and the vast Bavarian National Museum (www.bayerisches-nationalmuseum.de) are close by.

▲Deutsches Museum (Main Branch)

The museum's main Isar River location is halfway through a complete, multiyear overhaul. The first of two new wings opened recently with

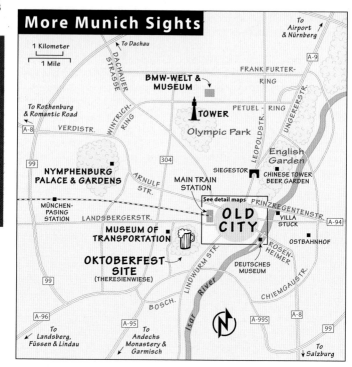

More Munich Sights

1 Kilometer
1 Mile

To Dachau

To Rothenburg & Romantic Road

To Airport & Nürnberg

FRANKFURTER-RING

A-9

BMW-WELT & MUSEUM

TOWER

Olympic Park

PETUEL - RING

DACHAUER STRASSE

WINTRICH-RING

VERDISTR.

A-8

99

NYMPHENBURG PALACE & GARDENS

304

ARNULF STR.

SIEGESTOR

English Garden

CHINESE TOWER BEER GARDEN

LEOPOLDSTR.

UNGERERSTR.

MAIN TRAIN STATION

MÜNCHEN-PASING STATION

LANDSBERGERSTR.

See detail maps

OLD CITY

PRINZREGENTENSTR.

VILLA STUCK

A-94

MUSEUM OF TRANSPORTATION

OKTOBERFEST SITE (THERESIENWIESE)

99

LINDWURM STR.

DEUTSCHES MUSEUM

ROSEN-HEIMER

OSTBAHNHOF

CHIEMGAUSTR.

BOSCH.

Isar River

A-96

A-95

A-995

A-8

99

To Landsberg, Füssen & Lindau

To Andechs Monastery & Garmisch

To Salzburg

fully redesigned exhibits. Themes include robotics, aviation, agriculture, health, film and imaging, motors, nuclear physics, hydraulic engineering, musical instruments, and more—the museum's collections are tremendously broad. Even those on roller skates will need to be selective. Study the floor plan and choose which sections interest you. Several exhibits are geared toward children, and there is a separate "Kids' Kingdom" for children ages 3-8. Everything in the museum is described in both English and German.

The other half of the museum's exhibits are currently closed but will open after a second stage of renovation, projected to end in 2028.

▶ €14, €29 family ticket, €3 extra for planetarium show, daily 9:00-17:00,

Chinese Tower in the English Garden

An early computer in the Deutsches Museum

ask for the English map, several small cafés in and around the museum, nice gift shop, +49 89 217 9333, www.deutsches-museum.de.

Getting There: Take the U-1, U-2, or tram #18 to Fraunhoferstrasse, then walk down to the river and turn left down a long block to the corner of Corneliusstrasse. Enter from the bridge (Corneliusbrücke). You can also take bus #52 or #62 to the Baaderstrasse stop, which is just across the intersection from the museum gate.

Near the Oktoberfest Grounds
▲Museum of Transportation (Verkehrszentrum)
This fun museum has enough to interest the casual visitor—and is heaven for any driving enthusiast. You'll see all aspects of transport, from old big-wheeled bikes to Benz's first car (a three-wheeler from the 1880s) to sleek ICE super-trains. The museum is part of the Deutsches Museum but has a separate ticket.

▶ *€7, €15 family ticket, daily 9:00-17:00; take the U-4 or U-5 to Schwanthalerhöhe, museum is a few steps away at Am Bavariapark 5, +49 89 217 9333, www.deutsches-museum.de/verkehrszentrum.*

Outside the City Center
▲BMW-Welt and Museum
At the headquarters of BMW ("bay-em-VAY," to Germans), Beamer dreamers can visit two space-age buildings to learn more about this brand's storied heritage.

The **BMW-Welt showroom**—a cloud-shaped, glass-and-steel architectural masterpiece—is reason enough to visit. It's free to enter and filled with exhibits designed to fuel potential customers' dreams.

In addition to touch-screen stations, high-powered videos, and an inviting cafeteria, you'll see the newest models and get a breathtaking look at the future.

Across the swoopy bridge at the far end of BMW-Welt is the futuristic, bowl-shaped **museum.** It encloses a world of floating walkways linking exhibits on BMW design and technology through the years—from airplane engines to motorcycles, followed by the first BMW sedan in 1929. Dozens of real cars and motorcycles of every era and type are on display—the 1956 BMW 507 is enough to rev almost anyone's engine.

At basement level, a worthwhile **Remembrance** exhibit focuses on the Nazi period, when BMW produced weapons and used forced labor, and the company's ongoing efforts to make amends.

▶ *Museum—€10, online ticket purchase encouraged, €3 discount with Olympic Park or Gray Line ticket—also applies to tours, open Tue-Sun 10:00-18:00, closed Mon; BMW-Welt showroom—free, building open daily until 24:00, exhibits staffed 9:00-20:00; +49 89 125 016 001, www.bmw-welt.com.*

Tours: Museum—€13, 1 hour; BMW-Welt showroom—€8, 40 minutes; factory—€14, 1.5 hours, ages 6 and up, best to book well in advance. Reservations must be made by phone at +49 89 125 016 001 or email at infowelt@bmw-welt.com; see website for details.

Getting There: Ride the U-3 to Olympia-Zentrum and follow signs for *BMW-Welt/BMW Museum.* As you exit, ahead is the BMW-Welt entry, the massive multicornered building across the street to your left is the BMW factory, the quadruple "piston" towers are the corporate offices, and the BMW Museum is in the half-visible gray

The Museum of Transportation

BMW-Welt is a fancy car showroom.

"soup bowl." On a bike, it's easily reached, and well signed, from the English Garden.

Olympic Park (Olympiapark München) and TV Tower (Olympiaturm)

Munich hosted the 1972 Olympics. Today the grounds are worthwhile for the pleasant park, striking "cobweb"-style stadium, 620-foot view TV tower (Olympiaturm), and excellent swimming pool.

▶ Tower—€11, €10 with BMW Museum ticket, daily 9:00-23:00, +49 89 3067 2750, www.olympiapark.de; pool—€6, daily 7:00-23:00, +49 89 2361 5050, www.swm.de. The U-3 runs from Marienplatz directly to the Olympia-Zentrum stop.

Day Trips from Munich

Munich's best day trips are Neuschwanstein Castle and Salzburg (see those chapters), but there are other sights within striking distance.

Nürnberg, easily reached by fast train (2/hour, 1 hour), is known for its glorious medieval architecture, haunting Nazi past, important

The BMW Museum (with the Olympic Park tower behind) displays stylish cars in modern buildings.

Andechs Monastery serves up some of the best beer in Germany in a serene rural setting.

Germanic history museum, and Germany's tiniest bratwurst (www.tourismus.nuernberg.de).

The **Andechs Monastery** offers a fine Baroque church in a rural Bavarian setting at a monastery that serves hearty cafeteria-quality food—and perhaps the best beer in Germany. To get there (75 minutes), take the S-8 to Herrsching, and catch bus #951 (free to enter, beer garden open Mon-Fri 11:00-20:00, Sat-Sun from 10:00, +49 8152 376 261, www.andechs.de).

If you have more time, the **Romantic Road bus** (May-Sept only) is a slow, scenic joyride that connects Munich's central bus station (ZOB) to several cute towns as it makes its way through Dinkelsbühl, Rothenburg, Würzburg, Frankfurt, and other destinations en route (schedule at www.romantischestrasse.de).

Activities

You'll never run out of things to do in Munich. This chapter offers suggestions for tours, shopping, and evening entertainment. Bike and walking tours range from the traditional city walk to sudsy beer tours. For a relaxing day, rent a bike to enjoy the English Garden, or pedal along the river to outlying sights. I've listed some concert and music options, but many prefer to spend Munich evenings in a frothy beer hall or outdoor beer garden (see the Eating chapter for suggestions).

TOURS

🎧 To sightsee on your own, download my free **Munich City Walk audio tour** (see sidebar on page 11 for details).

Hop-On, Hop-Off Bus Tour

Gray Line tours leave from Karlsplatz 21. Choose between a basic, one-hour "Express" route that heads past the Pinakotheks and Marienplatz (€20, departs daily 10:00-16:00) and the "Grand" route that lasts 2.5 hours (€25, departs daily 10:00-16:30, adds Nymphenburg and the BMW center). Booking online gets you a small discount (+49 89 5490 7560, www.stadtrundfahrten-muenchen.de).

Walking Tours

Radius Tours runs a daily city tour (€16, at 10:15, 2.5 hours) and a "Third Reich Tour" (€23, daily at 15:00, off-season daily at 11:30, 2.5 hours). They also offer an educational "Munich Bavarian Beer Tour" (€47; Mon-Sat 18:00, off-season Tue, Thu, and Sat at 18:00; 3.5 hours). During Oktoberfest, they run an Oktoberfest tour instead—reserve well in advance. All tours depart from the Radius office near the train station at Dachauer Strasse 4 (RS%—use the "student rate" when booking online; office open daily 8:30-18:00, Nov-March until 14:00, +49 89 543 487 7740, www.radiustours.com). Advance booking is recommended and easiest online.

Local Guides

Each of these guides can meet you at your hotel and tailor a visit to your interests: **Michael and Birgit Borio** (brother-and-sister team;

See the sights on a hop-on, hop-off bus...

...or by joining a guided walking tour.

€170/3 hours, email to make a plan or explore a longer tour; Michael: +49 173 700 4633, michbo@web.de; Birgit: +49 173 319 1565, bborio@yahoo.de); **Georg Reichlmayr** (€210/3 hours, +49 8131 86800, mobile +49 170 341 6384, www.muenchen-stadtfuehrung.de); **Birgit Stempfle** (€210/3 hours, +49 171 718 1465, www.sightseeing-munich.de); and **Paul Riedel** (€280/half-day, €390/full day, has a car for up to six, +49 089 747 47493, www.paul-riedel.de).

Bike Tours

Both of these outfits offer discounts to my readers (tours often fill, so reservations are smart): **Radius Tours** (RS%—select the "student rate" when booking online; April-Oct daily at 10:00, no tours off-season, see contact info above) and **Mike's Bike Tours** (RS%, 4 hours, 1-hour break in Chinese Tower beer garden, daily at 11:30, meet under tower of Old Town Hall, +49 89 2554 3987, www.mikesbiketours.com).

Self-Guided Isar River Bike Ride: Here's an easy, scenic ride you can do on your own. Munich's river, lined by a gorgeous park, leads bikers into the pristine countryside in just a few minutes. From downtown (easy access from the English Garden or Deutsches Museum), follow the riverside bike path south (upstream) along the east (left) bank. You can't get lost. Just stay on the lovely bike path. It crosses the

Level and compact, Munich is great by bike.

river after a while, passing tempting little beer gardens. Go as far as you like, then retrace your route to get home. The closest bike rental is Mike's Bike Tours (see above).

Self-Guided Ride to Nymphenburg, Olympic Park, and BMW: For another great city ride, take the bike path along Arnulfstrasse, pedaling out to Nymphenburg Palace. Then head to Olympic Park and the BMW sights, and finish at the English Garden (for the late-afternoon or early-evening scene) before returning to the center.

SHOPPING

While the whole city is great for shopping, the most glamorous area is around Marienplatz. Here are a few stores and streets to consider.

Bavarian Souvenirs: Servus Heimat's amusing shop at the Munich City Museum is a good source of unusual gifts that remind Bavarians of their childhood (Tue-Fri 13:00-18:00, Sat-Sun from 12:00, closed Mon; tucked between the City Museum and the Stadt Café at St.-Jakobs-Platz 1, +49 89 2370 2380, www.servusheimat.com). For fine-quality (and very expensive) dirndls and lederhosen, head to **Loden-Frey Verkaufshaus** (Mon-Sat 10:00-19:00, closed Sun, a block west of Marienplatz at Maffeistrasse 7, +49 89 210 390, www.loden-frey.com). For less expensive (but still good quality) traditional gear, visit **Angermaier Trachten,** near the Viktualienmarkt (Mon-Fri 11:00-19:00, Sat 10:00-17:00, closed Sun, Rosental 10, +49 89 2300 0199, www.trachten-angermaier.de). **Gottseidank,** across from St. Peter's Church, sells dressy, up-to-date Bavarian sweaters and jackets (Mon-Fri 10:30-18:30, Sat until 19:00, closed Sun, Petersplatz 8, www.gottseidank.com). **Obletter,** right on Karlsplatz, has wooden toys and a fun section full of puppets (Mon-Sat 10:00-20:00, closed Sun, Karlsplatz 11, +49 89 5508 9510).

Window Shopping and Malls: Stroll from **Marienplatz** down the pedestrianized **Weinstrasse** (to the left as you face the New Town Hall). Look for **Fünf Höfe** on your left, a delightful indoor/outdoor mall filled with Germany's top shops (https://fuenfhoefe.de). Even if you're not a shopper, wander through the **Kunsthalle** to appreciate the architecture, the elegant window displays, and the sight of Bavarians living very well. The nearby **Maximilianstrasse** is home to Munich's most exclusive shops.

Bavarian souvenirs, from traditional to quirky   Munich nightlife—theater, music, and beer

Department Stores: Ludwig Beck, an upscale department store at Marienplatz, has been a local institution since 1861 (designer clothing, music, stationery, cosmetics, and fine fabrics). For more reasonable prices near Marienplatz, try Galeria Kaufhof (midrange; sells everything), or C&A (cheap yet respectable; sells only clothing).

VAT and Customs

Getting a VAT Refund: If you purchase more than €25 worth of goods at a single store, you may be eligible to get a refund of the 19 percent value-added tax (VAT). Get more details from your merchant or see RickSteves.com/vat.

Customs for American Shoppers: You can take home $800 worth of items per person duty-free, once every 31 days. You can bring in one liter of alcohol duty-free. For details on allowable goods, customs rules, and duty rates, visit Help.cbp/gov.

NIGHTLIFE

On a balmy evening under the stars or in a cozy cellar with friendly locals, it's hard to beat the beer-and-oompah beer hall scene, but be sure to explore other options.

Tickets: Check the München Ticket website to see what's on (www.muenchenticket.de), or try calling +49 89 5481 8181.

Music and Dance: Ballet and opera fans can check the schedule at the **Bayerisch Staatsoper,** centrally located next door to the Residenz. These shows are popular, so book at least two months ahead—seats range from reasonable to very pricey (Max-Joseph-Platz

2, +49 89 2185 1920, www.staatsoper.de). The **Hotel Bayerischer Hof**'s nightclub has live music—major jazz acts plus pop/soul/disco—in a posh, dress-up, expensive setting (Promenadeplatz 2, +49 89 212 0994, www.bayerischerhof.de). **Café am Beethovenplatz** is another option for live classical, jazz, and swing music. For familiar Broadway-style musicals (usually in German), try the **Deutsches Theater** (Schwanthalerstrasse 13, +49 89 5523 4444, www.deutsches-theater. de).

Pubs: Giesinger Bräu has a little stand-up only outpost (called *Stehausschank*), with hipster beer and a hipster crowd, facing the Viktualienmarkt (Tue-Thu 14:00-22:00, Fri-Sat from 11:00, across from Der Pschorr at Prälat-Zistl-Strasse 4, www.giesinger-braeu.de). **Jodlerwirt** ("Yodeling Innkeeper") is a cellar pub billing itself as "the place where the world meets Bavaria" (Tue-Sat 17:00-late, closed Sun-Mon except during festivals, live music Thu-Sat, near the Old Town Hall, just off Marienplatz, at Tal 1, +49 89 221 249, www.jodler-wirt. com). **Kennedy's Irish Pub** is a high-energy music and sports bar at Sendlinger Tor with nightly music from 22:00 (Sendlinger-Tor-Platz 11, +49 89 5998 8460, www.kennedysmunich.de). **Gärtnerplatz** is a good, untouristed area known for its nightlife—both gay and straight (a 30-minute walk due south of Marienplatz; bus #52 from Marienplatz, or U-1 or U-2 to Fraunhoferstrasse).

Sleeping

Unless you hit Munich during a fair, convention, or big holiday, you can find a fine double room with breakfast in a good basic hotel for €100. Student hotels around the main train station house anyone who's young at heart for as low as €25.

Most of my accommodations are in two main areas: not far from the station, and in the old center, between Marienplatz and Sendlinger Tor. Most hotels here have slippery pricing schemes. During major conventions and events, prices increase from 20 percent to as much as 300 percent. To save money, or if the central area is booked, search online for a reliable chain hotel near an outlying U-Bahn, S-Bahn, or tram stop.

Munich Hotels

I like places that are clean, central, relatively quiet at night, reasonably priced, friendly, small enough to have a hands-on owner or manager, and run with a respect for German traditions. I'm more impressed by a handy location and fun-loving philosophy than oversized TVs and a fancy gym. Most of my recommendations fall short of perfection. But if I can find a place with most of these features, it's a keeper.

Hotels and B&Bs are sometimes located on the higher floors of a multipurpose building with a secured door. Hotel elevators are common, though small, and some older buildings still lack them. You may have to climb a flight of stairs to reach the elevator (if so, you can ask the front desk for help carrying your bags up).

Many hotels and pensions include breakfast in the room price and pride themselves on laying out an attractive buffet spread. (However, some hotels let you choose whether to pay extra for breakfast.) Even if you're not a big breakfast eater, take advantage of the buffet to fortify yourself for the day. Expect sliced bread, rolls, pastries, cereal, yogurt (both plain and with fruit), eggs, cold cuts, cheese, and fruit. You'll always find coffee, tea, and some sort of *Saft* (juice).

Making Reservations

Reserve your rooms as soon as you've pinned down your travel dates. Book your room directly via email or phone or through the hotel's official website. The hotelier wants to know:

- Type(s) of room(s) you want and number of guests
- Number of nights you'll stay
- Arrival and departure dates, written European-style as day/month (18/06 or 18 June)
- Special requests (en suite bathroom, cheapest room, twin beds vs. double bed, quiet room)
- Applicable discounts (such as a Rick Steves discount, cash discount, or promotional rate)

Most places will request a credit-card number to hold your room. If the hotel's website doesn't have a secure form where you can enter the number directly, share this info via a phone call.

If you must cancel, it's courteous—and smart—to do so with as much notice as possible. Cancellation policies can be strict; read the fine print before you book.

Always call or email to reconfirm your room reservation a few

Sleep Code

Dollar signs reflect average rates for a standard double room with breakfast in high season.

$$$$	**Splurge:** Most rooms over €190
$$$	**Pricier:** €150-190
$$	**Moderate:** €110-150
$	**Budget:** €70-110
¢	**Backpacker:** Under €70
RS%	**Rick Steves discount**

Unless otherwise noted, credit cards are accepted, hotel staff speak basic English, and free Wi-Fi is available. If the listing includes **RS%**, request a Rick Steves discount.

days in advance. For B&Bs or very small hotels, I call again on my arrival day to tell my host what time to expect me (especially important if arriving after 17:00).

Budget Tips

Comparison-shop by checking prices at several hotels (on each hotel's own website, on a booking site, or by email). For the best deal, *book directly with the hotel.* Ask for a discount if paying in cash.

Guesthouses—the German equivalent to B&Bs—are small, warm, family-run accommodations. Known as *Pensionen, Gasthäuser,* or *Gasthöfe* in German, they give you double the cultural intimacy for half the price. The smallest establishments are private homes with rooms (*Zimmer*). Finding and booking a guesthouse is no different than reserving a hotel, but a direct booking is especially appreciated at mom-and-pop places, and will likely net you a better price.

A short-term rental—whether an apartment, a house, or a room in a private residence—is a popular alternative, especially if you plan to settle in one location for several nights. For stays longer than a few days, you can usually find a rental that's comparable to—and cheaper than—a hotel room with similar amenities. Websites such as Airbnb, FlipKey, Booking.com, and VRBO let you browse a wide range of properties. Alternatively, rental agencies such as InterhomeUSA.com and RentaVilla.com can provide a more personalized service (their curated listings are also more expensive).

SOUTH OF THE TRAIN STATION
Multicultural area with Munich's highest concentration of hotels and lower prices than the old city center. Some parts have gentrified, but pockets of vice remain.

$$$ Hotel Schiller5 Dark wood elegance, most rooms come with kitchenette, family rooms, air-con, elevator, coin-op laundry, pay parking—reserve.

Schillerstrasse 5, +49 89 515 040, www.schiller5.com

$$$ Hotel Marc München Polished, modern, refined lobby, classy breakfast spread, RS%, air-con, elevator, pay parking.

Senefelderstrasse 12, +49 89 559 820, www.hotel-marc.de

$$ Hotel Cocoon Hauptbahnhof Rustic countryside/alpine theme, breakfast extra, air-con, bike rental, pay parking.

Mittererstrasse 9, +49 89 5999 3905, www.cocoon-hotels.de

$$ Arthotel Arty lobby, very normal rooms, stop across street for bus #58 to Königsplatz and museum district, air-con, pay parking.

Paul-Heyse-Strasse 10, +49 89 592 122, www.arthotelmunich.de

$$ Hotel Europäischer Hof Huge, impersonal hotel with decent rooms, RS%, includes breakfast when you book direct, elevator, pay parking.

Bayerstrasse 31, +49 89 551 510, www.heh.de

$$ Helvetia Hotel Functional rooms, decorated with pop art, breakfast extra, air-con, elevator, smoking rooms available.

Schillerstrasse 6, +49 89 590 6850, www.helvetia-hotel.com

¢ CVJM (YMCA) Open to all ages; clean, slick, and simple rooms each with its own bathroom, family rooms available, air-con.

landwehrstrasse 13, +49 89 552 1410, www.cvjm-muenchen.org

¢ Wombat's Hostel Hip and colorful; dorms are fresh, modern, and equipped with bathrooms; bright rooms facing winter garden have huge windows, family rooms, laundry.

Senefelderstrasse 1, +49 89 5998 9180, www.wombats-hostels.com/munich

NORTH OF THE TRAIN STATION
Five-minute walk north of the train station, by the Karlstrasse tram stop. Slightly more gentrified than south side.

$$ Augusten Hotel Modern rooms in a handsome corner building.

Augustenstrasse 2, +49 89 516 8900, www.augustenhotel.com

$ The Ibis München City Impersonal chain hotel, predictable rooms, gambling parlor next door, air-con.

Dachauer Strasse 21, +49 89 551 930, https://ibis.accor.com

NEAR THE OKTOBERFEST GROUNDS

Safe-feeling, manicured residential neighborhood. Near the Theresienwiese U-Bahn stop, within a block or two of the Oktoberfest grounds, about a 15-minute walk from the train station.

$$$ Hotel Uhland Stately mansion, rooms have old-style character and modern bathrooms, family rooms, elevator, limited pay parking.

Uhlandstrasse 1, +49 89 543 350, www.hotel-uhland.de

IN THE OLD CENTER

This area south of Marienplatz (between Sendlinger Tor and Isartor) feels more genteel. Convenient for sightseeing.

$$$$ Derag Livinghotel am Viktualienmarkt Two connected buildings: one elegant with great views, the other with kitchenettes; breakfast extra, air-con, elevator, laundry facilities, parking discounts.

Frauenstrasse 4, +49 89 885 6560, www.living-hotels.com

$$$$ Hotel Blauer Bock Great location near Munich City Museum, contemporary rooms, top-notch breakfast, elevator, pay parking—reserve.

Sebastiansplatz 9, +49 89 231 780, www.hotelblauerbock.de

$$$ Mercure München Altstadt Hotel Reliable with modern comforts, business-class rooms, quiet street close to Marienplatz action, fine service, air-con.

Hotterstrasse 4, +49 89 232 590, www.mercure-muenchen-altstadt.de

$$$ Hotel am Viktualienmarkt Small but well designed, good-value single rooms, family rooms, apartment, table fans.

Utzschneiderstrasse 14, +49 89 231 1090, www.hotel-am-viktualienmarkt.de

$$$ Hotel am Markt Simple, tastefully renovated rooms; neighboring church's bells ring hourly, skip expensive breakfast, elevator.

Heiliggeiststrasse 6, +49 89 225 014, www.hotel-am-markt.eu

$$$ Hotel Isartor Comfortable rooms on six floors, close to Isartor and its S-Bahn stop, half the rooms have air-con, some have balconies.

Baaderstrasse 2, +49 89 216 3340, www.hotel-isartor.de

$$$ Hotel Admiral Classy yet homey, serves breakfast in back garden in good weather, air-con.

Kohlstrasse 9, +49 89 216 350, www.hotel-admiral.de

$$ Motel One Sendlinger Tor Huge, inexpensive but posh-feeling, modern but tight rooms—some with views, breakfast extra, air-con, pay parking.

Herzog-Wilhelm-Strasse 28, +49 89 5177 7250, www.motel-one.com

Eating

Munich is often voted one of Germany's most livable cities, and one of the reasons is the city's appreciation for good food and drink in casual settings. Munich's best-known food option is the traditional beer hall. These can range from rowdy oompah wurst factories to under-the-stars beer gardens to elegant restaurants. But Munich also has other dining opportunities. You'll find both budget take-out places and top-notch international cuisine.

My listings are either in the Old Town (within a 10-minute walk of Marienplatz), in the convenient train station neighborhood, or in the English Garden. No matter where you dine, expect it to be *gemüt-lich*—a much-prized Bavarian virtue, meaning an atmosphere of relaxed coziness.

When in Germany

I eat on the German schedule. For breakfast, I eat at the hotel (fresh-baked bread, meat, cheese, Müsli cereal) or grab a pastry and coffee at a bakery. Traditionally, the German lunch (12:00–14:00) has been a big meal (and many restaurants offer lunch specials), though busy Germans today might just grab a sandwich at a bakery. Many Germans are health-conscious and quite passionate about choosing organic (*Bio*) products, but many starchy, high-fat, high-calorie traditional foods remain staples.

In between meals, you could stop at a take-out stand for a wurst. Bavarians even have a special word for the traditional in-between-meal snack—*Brotzeit* ("bread time")—a platter of bread with cold cuts, cheese, and pickles. In the late afternoon, Germans enjoy a beverage with friends at an outdoor table on a lively square. Dinner (18:00–21:00) is the time for slowing down and savoring a quiet multicourse restaurant meal, or combining dinner with beer and fun in a beer hall.

Restaurant Etiquette

Full-service, sit-down restaurants in Germany operate much like restaurants everywhere, but there are a few small differences in etiquette.

You only need to tip at restaurants that have table service. If you order your food at a counter, don't tip. At restaurants with wait staff, it's common to tip after a good meal by rounding up (roughly 10 percent). Rather than leaving coins behind on the table (considered slightly rude), Germans usually pay directly: When the server comes by with the bill, simply hand over paper money, stating the total you'd like to pay. For example, if paying for a €10 meal with a €20 bill, while handing your money to the server, say "Eleven, please" (or *"Elf, bitte"* if you've got your German numbers down). The server will keep a €1 tip and give you €9 in change.

Germans are willing to pay for bottled water with their meal (*Mineralwasser mit/ohne Gas*—with/without carbonation). You can request tap water (*Leitungswasser*), though your server may grumble. A *Stammtisch* sign hanging over a table means it's reserved for regulars. Many eateries offer pleasant outdoor seating in good weather. Bavarian eateries are officially smoke-free indoors.

Some restaurants offer inexpensive €7-10 weekday hot-lunch specials that aren't listed on the regular menu (look for the *Tageskarte* or *Tagesangebot,* or just ask—sometimes available at dinner, too). For

Restaurant Code

Dollar signs reflect the cost of a typical main course.

$$$$	**Splurge:** Most main courses over €25
$$$	**Pricier:** €20-25
$$	**Moderate:** €15-20
$	**Budget:** Under €15

A wurst stand or other takeout spot is **$**; a beer hall, Biergarten, or basic sit-down eatery is **$$**; a casual but more upscale restaurant is **$$$**; and a swanky splurge is **$$$$**.

smaller portions, order from the *kleine Hunger* (small hunger) section of the menu. Simple dishes of wurst with sauerkraut and bread are about €7-9.

Once you're seated, take your time—only a rude server will rush you. Good service is relaxed (slow to an American). To wish others "Happy eating!" offer a cheery *"Guten Appetit!"* When you want the bill, say, *"Die Rechnung, bitte"* (dee REHKH-noong, BIT-teh).

Bakeries, Cafés, and More

Besides fancy restaurants, these less-formal places will fill the tank.

Other Restaurants: Places that serve meals go by many names. *Gasthaus, Gasthof, Gaststätte,* and *Gaststube* all loosely describe an informal, inn-type eatery. A *Kneipe* is a bar, and a *Keller* (or *Ratskeller*) is an eatery located in a cellar. A beer hall (*Brauhaus*), beer garden (*Biergarten*), or wine cellar (*Weinstube*) will serve basic, traditional meals. Department-store cafeterias (usually on the top floor with a view) are handy.

Cheap Take-out Meals and Picnics: Many Bavarians go to a bakery (*Bäckerei*) for a good, cheap sandwich. Bakeries don't offer full sit-down meals, but they usually have a few tables.

Munich makes it easy to turn a picnic into a first-class affair. Grab something to go and enjoy a bench in a lively square or leafy park. Some beer gardens allow patrons who order a drink to picnic at their tables. It's easy to find premade sandwiches, take-out salads, and cold cuts at bakeries, butcher shops (*Metzgerei*), and supermarkets. A

Schnellimbiss—or simply *Imbiss*—is a small fast-food takeaway stand where you can get a bratwurst and more.

Best of the Wurst: In Germany, you're never far from a *Würstchenbude* (sausage stand; *Würstelstand* in Austria). The wurst, usually pork sausage, comes in many varieties. *Bratwurst* is a generic term that simply means "sausage for grilling or frying." There's also *Bockwurst, Leberwurst,* and so on. Generally, the darker the weenie, the spicier it is. Munich's best-known specialty—often available only until noon—is *Weisswurst:* White-colored veal sausage (peel off the skin before you eat it), served with sweet mustard and a pretzel.

Your wurst usually comes with a roll (*Semmel*) and possibly your choice of a slice of bread (*Brot*), a pretzel, or—in restaurants—potato salad. Sauces include mustard—sweet (*süss*) or sharp (*scharf*), ketchup, curry-ketchup, and more.

Snack Foods: Pretzels (*Brezeln*), either plain or buttered, make for an inexpensive snack. *Obatzda* is a soft cheese spread with paprika and often garlic or onions that's eaten on bread.

Global Cuisine: All schnitzeled out? An Asian rice or noodle dish, a freshly baked pizza, or a Turkish sandwich will cost you about €4-7. Originally from Turkey, *döner kebab* (gyro-like, pita-wrapped rotisserie meat) is a classic take-out meal for Germans. Turkish cafés also sell falafel (chickpea croquettes), "Turkish pizzas," and much more.

Beer Halls and Beer Gardens

One of Munich's great experiences is drinking some of the world's best beer in a vast indoor beer hall or outdoor beer garden—many establishments offer both seating options. Here, the beer comes in big steins, meals are inexpensive, and surly servers quickly clear the tables. Closed days disappear during Oktoberfest, when most places are open daily.

Beer gardens began back when monks brewed beer, stored in cellars beneath courtyards kept cool by the shade of bushy chestnut trees. Eventually, tables were set up for the buying public, and these convivial eateries evolved.

Etiquette: Most beer halls are informal places where you can seat yourself, often at big shared tables. But don't sit at tables marked *Stammtisch*—they're reserved for regulars. Beer halls have a long

Turkish *döner kebabs* are everywhere.

A *Mass* of *Helles* is the classic beer order.

tradition as the social hub of the community. In the days before radio and TV, politicians came here to connect with the public.

Most beer gardens also have a deposit (*Pfand*) system for their big glass steins: You pay €1 extra, and when you're finished, you can take the mug and your deposit token (*Pfandmarke*) to the return person (*Pfandrückgabe*) for your refund. If you buy a bottled beer, pour it into the glass before you check out; otherwise you'll pay two deposits (one for the glass, the other for the bottle).

Many beer halls have a cafeteria system. If two prices are listed, *Selbstbedienung* is for self-service (*Bitte bedienen Sie sich selbst* means "please serve yourself"), while *Bedienung* is for table service. At a large beer garden, assemble your dream feast by visiting various counters—get your roast chicken here, your pork shoulder there, then head to the salad bar. After the meal, bus your dirty dishes at the station marked *Geschirrabgabe*.

Beer: The average German drinks 27 gallons of beer a year and has a tremendous variety to choose from. *Flaschenbier* is bottled, and *vom Fass* is on tap. Huge liter mugs of tap beer (called *eine Mass* in German) cost about €8. A half-liter is *eine Halbe*. In some places, if you order *eine Halbe*, the server might say, "Why don't you go home and come back when you're thirsty?"

Most Bavarian beers fall into four categories: *Helles Bier* is light in color but not "lite" in calories. *Dunkles Bier* is dark beer. Munich-style *dunkles* is sweet and malty. *Weissbier* (what Americans call "Hefeweizen") is a yeasty, wheat-based beer, with a frothy head, served in a tall glass with a lemon wedge. Other Bavarian specialties are *Bockbier* (a high-alcohol, hoppy, bittersweet amber) and

Märzenbier (a light, malty, and highly alcoholic lager brewed in March to be ready for Oktoberfest). A *Radler* is a refreshing half-lager, half-lemon soda and a *Diesel* mixes lager and cola.

Best Beer Places: For the classic cliché, nothing beats the rowdy Hofbräuhaus—the only beer hall where you'll actually find oompah music. Locals prefer beer gardens: try the Augustiner (near the train station), the Viktualienmarkt, or the English Garden. If you're in Munich in September through October, you can visit the biggest beer garden of them all—Oktoberfest. If you've had enough fun, beer-hall men's rooms come with vomitoriums.

Traditional Bavarian Cuisine

Traditional Bavarian cooking is heavy, hearty, meaty, and tasty. Sausage dishes are served with sauerkraut as an excuse for a vegetable. These days, however, health-conscious Germans are turning to lighter fare and organic *"Bio"* foods, and German chefs are adopting international influences to jazz up "Modern German" cuisine.

Main Dishes: The classic staple across Germany is sausage—hundreds of varieties of wursts, served with a roll or sauerkraut. Other common dishes are schnitzel—a meat cutlet that's been pounded flat, breaded, and fried—and pork knuckle (*Schweinshax'n*). A dish described as *Braten* can mean roasted, grilled, or fried—as in *Schweinebraten* (roasted pork), or *Bratwurst* (grilled sausage). For a meal-sized salad, order a *Salatteller*.

Besides these foods found all over Germany, there are some Bavarian specialties: *Dampfnudel* is a steamed bread roll with toppings, served as either a savory main dish or sweet dessert. A *Fleischpflanzerl* is a big meatball. *Steckerlfisch* is whole fish that's seasoned and grilled on a stick.

Meat and potatoes—traditional Bavarian food

Enjoy informal take-out stands.

Sides: Common side dishes include *Knödel* (dumplings), spaetzle (little noodles), potatoes, soups, and salads. *Spargel* (giant white asparagus) is a must in May-June. Germans make excellent salads—try a *grüner Salat* (mostly lettuce), *gemischter Salat* (lettuce and mixed vegetables), *Kartoffelsalat* (potato salad), or another option. Along with their beer, Bavarians enjoy a *Brezel* (pretzel) or a *Radi* (radish that's thinly spiral-cut and salted).

Drinks: Germans love their white wine, which is commonly sold by the deciliter (prices listed per 1 dl, about 3.5 ounces). You can order by the glass simply by asking for *ein Glas,* or to clarify that you don't want much, *eine Dezi* (one deciliter). For a mini-pitcher of wine, ask for *ein Viertel* (quarter-liter, about two glasses' worth). For a half-liter pitcher (about four glasses), request *ein Halber.* For white wine, ask for *Weisswein;* red wine is *Rotwein.* Order your wine *lieblich* (sweet), *halbtrocken* (medium), or *trocken* (dry). A *Weinschorle* is a spritzer of white wine pepped up with a little sparkling water. In winter, *Glühwein* (hot mulled wine) is popular.

The best-known white wines come from the Rhine and Mosel river valleys. Common grape varieties are Riesling (fruity, fragrant, elegant), *Gewürztraminer* ("spicy"), *Müller-Thurgau* (best when young), and *Liebfraumilch* ("beloved maiden's milk," a semisweet blending of varieties). From the region of Franconia (north of Munich)

Large beer halls often have various dining options—indoor, outdoor, waiters, or self-service.

comes *Grüner Silvaner,* an acidic, fruity white in a jug-shaped bottle. Germany is not known for its reds, but there's the velvety *Dornfelder* and the pinot noir-like *Spätburgunder.*

Even teetotalers can enjoy good-quality beers that are non-alcoholic (*"alkoholfreies Bier"*): lagers, *Weisses* (wheat-based), or *Malztrunk*—the sweet, dark, malted beverage that children quaff before they start drinking the real thing. Popular soft drinks include spritz drinks like *Apfelschorle* (apple juice and sparkling water) and *Spezi* (cola and orange soda).

Sweets: While you're sure to have *Apfelstrudel* (apple-pie filling wrapped in wafer-thin pastry), Germany offers much more. At a bakery (*Bäckerei*) or pastry shop (*Konditorei*) you'll find plenty of pastries, often with some kind of filling, like the *Krapfen,* a Bavarian jelly-filled doughnut. Gummi Bears from the German candy company Haribo are everywhere and taste better here close to the source. Ice-cream stores abound, often run by Italian immigrants. Get *eine Kugel*—a scoop—of your favorite and stroll the streets. Or join the Germans who enjoy sitting down with fancy sundaes in big bowls.

Guten Appetit!

ON OR NEAR MARIENPLATZ
These places are all within a 10-minute walk of Marienplatz.

1 **$$ Hofbräuhaus** World's most famous beer hall, grotesquely touristy but fun, oompah music, good for a large or light meal or just for a drink, decent food, seating areas from rowdy to mellow (daily 9:00-late).
Platzl 9, +49 89 290 136 100

2 **$$$ Altes Hackerhaus** Traditional, slightly fancy Bavarian fare, historic building with courtyard and interior nooks, Hacker-Pschorr beer (daily 10:30-24:00).
Sendlinger Strasse 14, +49 89 260 5026

3 **$$$ Brenner Grill** Fusion of northern Italian and southern German food; sprawling, high-energy place with big open grills; filled with locals (long hours Mon-Sat, closed Sun).
Maximilianstrasse 15, +49 89 452 2880

4 **$$$ Spatenhaus** Opera-goers' beer hall, elegant food in a rustic, traditional setting or outside on the square; reservations recommended for upstairs restaurant serving international cuisine (daily 9:30-23:00).
Residenzstrasse 12, +49 89 290 7060, www.spatenhaus.de

⑤ **$$$ Glockenspiel Café** Bird's-eye view of Marienplatz, good for coffee but go for the view more than the food, after 18:00 you must order dinner for view seating (Mon-Sat 9:00-24:00, Sun 10:00-19:00).
Marienplatz 28, +49 89 264 256

⑥ **$$ Blatt Salate** Great hideaway for a healthy lunch, order cafeteria-style, grab a table inside or out (Mon-Sat 11:00-19:00, closed Sun).
Schäfflerstrasse 7, +49 89 2102 0281

⑦ **$$ Pfälzer Residenz Weinstube** Traditional German dining hall in the Residenz complex, wine-friendly dishes and German wines by the tiny glass (daily 10:30-24:00).
Residenzstrasse 1, +49 89 225 628

IN OR NEAR THE VIKTUALIENMARKT
Colorful market a few steps south of Marienplatz.

⑧ **$ Die Münchner Suppenküche** Soup stand with picnic tables under a closed-in awning, self-service at the counter (Mon-Sat 10:00-18:00, closed Sun).
Near corner of Reichenbachstrasse and Blumenstrasse, +49 89 260 9599

⑨ **$ Teltschik's Wurststandl** Quick service, cheap local sausages (Tue-Sat 10:00-15:00, closed Sun-Mon).
Stand #17—near corner of Reichenbachstrasse and Blumenstrasse, +49 0172 134 9664

⑩ **$ Caspar Plautz** Enticing selection of baked potatoes *(Kartoffeln)* and fillings, take away or munch at tiny stand-up tables (Tue-Sat 8:00-17:00, closed Sun-Mon).
Stand #38, +49 179 663 2748

⑪ **$$$ Poseidon am Viktualienmarkt** Shiny stainless-steel eatery, fun and accessible seafood menu, indoor or outdoor seating, enticing self-service appetizer selection (Mon-Sat 11:00-18:00, closed Sun).
Westenriederstrasse 13, +49 89 299 296

⑫ **$$ Stadt Café** Lively, informal, and no-frills; sandwiches, vegetarian dishes, wine list, and cakes (Tue-Sun 11:00-22:00, closed Mon).
St.-Jakobs-Platz 1, +49 89 266 949

⑬ **$$ Eataly** Sparkling, pricey food court with seating inside and out (café open Mon-Sat 8:00-20:00, closed Sun; restaurants open Mon-Sat 12:00-22:00).
Blumenstrasse 4, +49 89 248 817 711

⑭ **$$ Sebastiansplatz Eateries** Many bistros lining pedestrianized, cobbled square—choose from French, Italian, Asian, or salads.
On Sebastiansplatz across from Schrannenhalle

$$$ Prinz Myshkin Vegetarian Restaurant Upscale vegetarian eatery, mod décor inside and quiet seating outside, enticing appetizer selection and tempting sweets, lunch specials (daily 11:00-23:00).

Hackenstrasse 2, +49 89 265 596

$$$ Der Pschorr Youthful, upscale beer hall with a view over the Viktualienmarkt, popular local brew in chilled glasses, organic "slow food" mixes modern and traditional, seasonal specials (daily 10:00-23:00).

Viktualienmarkt 15, +49 89 442 383 940

BREWERY RESTAURANTS AT THE FRAUENKIRCHE
Traditional fare and great beer at friendly prices in the shadow of the cathedral. All have characteristic interiors and fine tables outside.

 $$ Augustiner Klosterwirt Characteristic yet modern interior, delightful outdoor seating (daily until late).

Augustinerstrasse 1, +49 089 5505 4466

 $$ Andechser am Dom Behind the Frauenkirche, local favorite serving Andechs beer and great food, *Gourmetteller* sampler a hit, reserve during peak times (daily 10:00-24:00).

Frauenplatz 7, +49 89 2429 2920, www.andechser-am-dom.de

$$ Nürnberger Bratwurst Glöckl am Dom Traditional, fiercely Bavarian, popular with tourists, dine outside under trees or in the dark medieval interior, tasty *Nürnberger* sausages (daily 10:00-24:00).

Frauenplatz 9, +49 89 291 9450

NEAR THE TRAIN STATION
Less atmospheric neighborhood, but some good bargains and local feel.

 Augustiner Beer Garden Possibly Munich's best beer garden, sprawling under-the-leaves haven for locals on a nice summer evening, traditional food; $ self-service, $$ table service, or $$$ restaurant with more expensive dining (outdoor sections daily 11:00-24:00).

Arnulfstrasse 52, +49 89 594 393

$$ Park Café Beer Garden Bavarian food from self-service counters or modern indoor restaurant with a good-time bar menu and popular cocktails (daily 11:00-24:00).

Sophienstrasse 7, +49 89 5161 7980

 $$$ Münchner Stubn Traditional dishes with a modern twist, bright modern interior, lunch specials (daily 11:30-24:00).

Bayerstrasse 35, +49 89 551 113 330

㉓ **$$$ Café am Beethovenplatz** Inviting interior, charming garden; mix of Italian, Bavarian, and vegetarian fare; lunch specials, homemade cakes, live music (daily 10:00-24:00).

Goethestrasse 51, +49 89 552 9100

㉔ **$$$ La Vecchia Masseria** Pasta, pizzas, and seasonal Italian food served in a cozy Tuscan interior or flowery courtyard, reservations smart (daily 11:30-23:30).

Mathildenstrasse 3, +49 89 550 9090, www.lavecchiamasseria.de

㉕ **$$ Altin Dilim** Cafeteria-style Turkish food, handy pictorial menu, interesting decor, pay at counter (long hours daily).

Goethestrasse 17, +49 89 9734 0869

IN THE ENGLISH GARDEN

Outdoor ambience in sprawling public park. Most places are a 10-minute walk from any tram or U-Bahn stop.

㉖ **$$ Chinese Tower beer garden** Great for a balmy, relaxed evening; B.Y.O. food or buy from the cafeteria-style food counters; 6,000 seats, usually live music (in good weather Mon-Fri from 11:00, Sat-Sun from 10:00).

Englischer Garten 3, +49 89 383 8730

㉗ **$$$$ Seehaus Restaurant** Dressy and snobbish but worth the effort to find, locals love idyllic lakeside setting or classy indoors, excellent Mediterranean and Bavarian cooking, reservations wise (daily until late).

Kleinhesselohe 3, +49 89 381 6130, www.kuffler.de

㉘ **$$ Seehaus Beer Garden** Adjacent to Seehaus restaurant with same waterfront atmosphere in a casual setting, traditional beer-hall fare (daily 11:30-22:00 in good weather).

Kleinhesselohe 3, +49 89 381 6130

Munich Restaurants

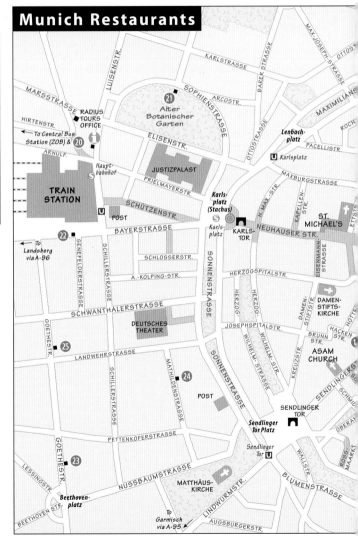

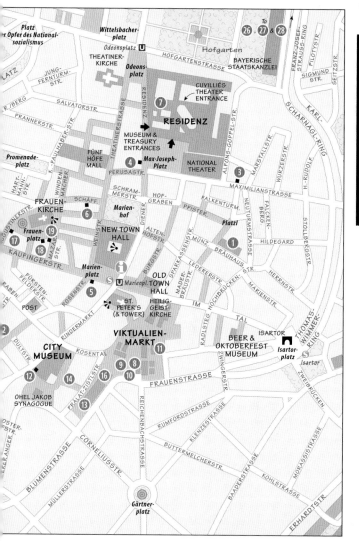

Einlass / entrance

465

nächste Touren / Next Tour

466 - 13:30
467 - 13:35
468 - 13:40

get your audioguide after the entra

Uhrzeit / time

13:26

Neuschwanstein Castle
& a Bit of Bavaria

Europe's most spectacular castle lies 80 miles southwest of
Munich. Perched dramatically on a hill, with its proud white tur-
rets, it's impressive inside and out. This chapter focuses on seeing
Neuschwanstein Castle (noy-SHVAHN-shtine) on a day trip, either
on your own or with a tour. I also cover nearby options: the equally
historic Hohenschwangau Castle (hoh-en-SHVAHN-gow) and short
hikes with great alpine scenery.

With more time, you can stay overnight in the nearby town of
Füssen and explore more of Bavaria—a picturesque land of cute villages, painted buildings shared by cows and farmers, and locals who
still yodel when they're happy.

THE KING'S CASTLES

Orientation

Cost: Timed-entry tour tickets for Neuschwanstein are €17.50, €2.50 for kids under 18; Hohenschwangau's are €23.50, €13.50 for kids 7-17, €2.50 for kids 6 and under (prices include online booking fee). A Königsticket combo-ticket for both castles is usually available for about €37.

Hours and Entry Times: The ticket center is open daily (8:00-16:00, phones open Mon-Fri 9:00-12:00 & 13:30-15:00). The first tour departs at 9:00 (usually 10:00 off-season); the last tour departs at 18:00 (15:30 off-season).

All tickets come with admission times. If you miss your appointed tour time, you can't get in. To tour both castles, try to do Hohenschwangau first. Allow at least two hours between your castle tour bookings. With a combo-ticket, you'll choose two entry times: one for Hohenschwangau and one for Neuschwanstein—keeping in mind that the Hohenschwangau tour lasts up to 45 minutes and the Neuschwanstein tour 30 minutes. If you're planning to hike up to Mary's Bridge prior to your Neuschwanstein

All Neuschwanstein tickets come with an entry time--don't miss it.

tour, allow plenty of time: There's often a line to get onto the bridge for that famous view.

Information: +49 8362 930 830, www.hohenschwangau.de.

Advance Tickets: It's smart to buy advance tickets online, particularly for holidays and weekends during peak season (June-Oct—especially July-Aug). Arrive well before your appointed entry time, as it takes a while to get up to the castles. If you know a few hours in advance that you're running late, call the office: They may be able to rebook you.

Tickets On-Site: A percentage of castle tickets are set aside for in-person purchase; arrive between 8:00 and 8:30; these tickets can sell out as early as 9:30.

Services: A TI (run by knowledgeable Thomas), bus stop, ATM, pay WC, lockers, and post machine cluster around the main intersection a couple hundred yards before you get to the ticket office (TI open daily 10:00-17:30, Nov-March Sat-Sun until 16:00, closed Mon-Fri, +49 8362 81980, www.schwangau.de). While the tiny bathrooms inside the castles themselves are free, you'll pay to use the WCs elsewhere.

Eating: I prefer to bring a packed lunch. The park by the Alpsee (the nearby lake) is ideal for a picnic, although you're not allowed to sit on the grass—only on the benches. You can find decent German fare at the snack stand across from the TI or next to Hotel Alpenstuben (between the TI and ticket center).

Getting Up to the Castles

From the ticket booth, Hohenschwangau is an easy 10-minute **walk** up the paved path past the bus parking (for a quicker ascent zigzag up to the big yellow castle using the ramp/stairs behind Hotel Müller). Neuschwanstein is a moderately steep, 30-minute hike in the other direction (also well signed—the most direct and least steep approach begins across the street from Hotel Müller).

You can take a **shuttle bus** to Neuschwanstein or a horse-drawn carriage. Neither option gets you to the castle doorstep. The shuttle bus departs about every 20 minutes from the bus stop next to the #4 parking lot just below Hohenschwangau and drops you off near Mary's Bridge (Marienbrücke), leaving you a steep, 10-minute downhill walk to the castle—be sure to see the view from Mary's Bridge before hiking down (€3 uphill, €2 downhill, €3.50 round-trip). **Horse-drawn**

Getting to King's Castles

The castles and nearby sights are two hours from Munich by train or car. The easiest way to see the castles is by booking a guided tour: It gets you there and back in a single day, and includes an English-speaking guide and reserved castle entry. But the castles are also completely doable on your own. Here are your options:

On Your Own by Train and Bus: From Munich, it's a two-hour train ride, followed by a 10-minute bus ride to the base of the castles.

If you're visiting both, reserve your ticket for Hohenschwangau first, choosing an afternoon slot (after 13:00). Book your Neuschwanstein tour two hours after your Hohenschwangau tour starts.

For this trip, get a Bayern-Ticket regional transit day pass (cheaper and covers bus between Füssen and the castles). The Bayern-Ticket is good for one day of unlimited travel for up to five people anywhere in Bavaria (plus Salzburg) for a low price (€26 for the first person plus €8 for each additional person). You can buy it online (www.bahn.com, look under "Regional Offers"); from ticket machines in stations or at public transit stops; or at train station ticket counters.

Note that on weekdays, the Bayern-Ticket is not valid before 9:00, and is valid only on slower "regional" trains—labeled on schedules as "BRB," "RB," "RE," or "IRE." For example, on weekdays the earliest train you can take to the castles with this ticket typically leaves Munich at 9:36, arriving direct in Füssen at 11:41. The connecting bus from Füssen station to the castles leaves at 12:05, arriving at 12:13 (check schedules in advance).

Rail pass-holders can use a pass day for the train to Füssen: Take whichever train you want, then pay €5 round-trip for the bus from Füssen to the castles, which doesn't accept rail passes. Be sure to check departure times for the last convenient bus-and-train connection from the castles back to Munich (it might be around 18:50, reaching Munich at 21:20).

By Rental Car: Note that road signs in the region refer to the sight as Königsschlösser. There's plenty of parking (all lots-€10). The first lots require more walking. The most convenient lot, by the lake (#4, Parkplatz am Alpsee), is up the small road past the souvenir shops and ticket center.

With a Bus Tour: For a little more money, an organized bus tour is a very convenient way to get from Munich to the King's Castles. You're guaranteed a seat (in summer, public transit to Neuschwanstein is routinely standing room only), you'll see more, your castle ticket is taken care of, and it's nice to have company and help.

Gray Line Tours offers an 11-hour bus tour to Neuschwanstein that also includes Ludwig's Linderhof Castle and 30 minutes in Oberammergau (€60, plus €30 for castle admission, reserve online, departs Karlsplatz daily at 8:30, +49 89 5490 7560, www.munichdaytrips. com). This tour can sell out, especially in summer, so it's wise to buy in advance.

Bus Bavaria (run by Mike's Bike Tours) offers a private bus tour for active travelers with a focus on the outdoors—a bike ride, hike, and short swim near Neuschwanstein are included (€59, RS%, does not include castle admission; advance booking recommended, check website for current times; meet at Mike's Bike Tours office near the Hofbräuhaus, Bräuhausstrasse 10—enter around corner on Hochbrückenstrasse, +49 89 2554 3987, www.mikesbiketours.com).

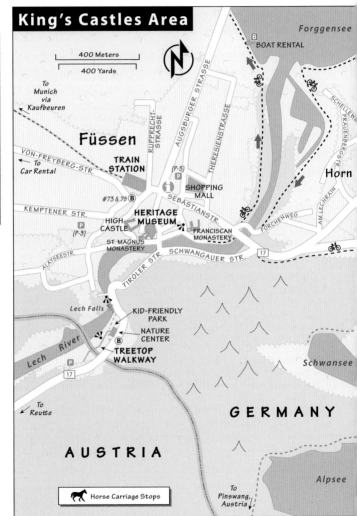

King's Castles Area

Forggensee

B BOAT RENTAL

400 Meters
400 Yards

N

To
Munich
via
Kaufbeuren

Füssen

RUPPRECHT-STRASSE

AUGSBURGER STRASSE

THERESIENSTRASSE

SCHELLEW
FRAUENBERGSTR.

VON-FREYBERG-STR.
To
Car Rental

**TRAIN
STATION**

(P-5)

Horn

KEMPTENER STR.

#73 & 78 **B**

SEBASTIANSTR.

**SHOPPING
MALL**

FORCHENWEG

AM LECHRAIN

**HIGH
CASTLE**

**HERITAGE
MUSEUM**

**FRANCISCAN
MONASTERY**

(P-3)

**ST. MAGNUS
MONASTERY**

ALATSEESTR.

TIROLER STR.

SCHWANGAUER STR.

17

Lech Falls

**KID-FRIENDLY
PARK**

Schwansee

**NATURE
CENTER**

B

**TREETOP
WALKWAY**

Lech River

17

To
Reutte

G E R M A N Y

A U S T R I A

Alpsee

To
Pinswang,
Austria

🐎 Horse Carriage Stops

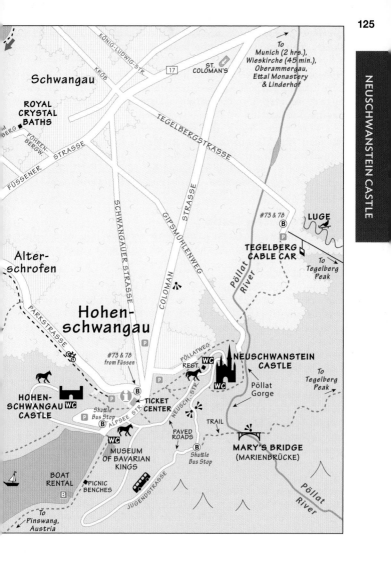

To Munich (2 hrs.),
Wieskirche (45 min.),
Oberammergau,
Ettal Monastery
& Linderhof

König-Ludwig-Str.

KROB

17

ST.
COLOMAN'S

Schwangau

ROYAL
CRYSTAL
BATHS

TEGELBERGSTRASSE

FÖHREN-
BERGW.
STRASSE

FÜSSENER STRASSE

#73 & 78

LUGE

TEGELBERG
CABLE CAR

To
Tegelberg
Peak

Alter-
schrofen

Pöllat River

SCHWANGAUER STRASSE

GIPSMÜHLENWEG

COLOMAN STRASSE

Hohen-
schwangau

PARKSTRASSE

P

#73 & 78
from Füssen

P

PÖLLATWEG

WC
REST.

NEUSCHWANSTEIN
CASTLE

WC

Pöllat
Gorge

To
Tegelberg
Peak

B

TICKET
CENTER

NEUSCH.-STR.

ALPSEE-STR.

HOHEN-
SCHWANGAU
CASTLE

WC

Shuttle
Bus Stop

P

B

WC

TRAIL

MUSEUM
OF BAVARIAN
KINGS

B

Shuttle
Bus Stop

PAVED
ROADS

MARY'S BRIDGE
(MARIENBRÜCKE)

BOAT
RENTAL

PICNIC
BENCHES

JUGENDSTRASSE

Pöllat River

B

To
Pinswang,
Austria

carriages, which leave across the street from Hotel Müller, are slower than walking and stop below Neuschwanstein, leaving you a five-minute uphill hike (€7 up, €3.50 down). Carriages also run to Hohenschwangau (€5.50 up, €3 down). Both buses and carriages can have long lines at peak times—especially if it's raining. You might wait up to 45 minutes—if you're cutting it close to your appointed time, you may need to hoof it.

With time, here's the most economical and least strenuous plan: Ride the bus to Mary's Bridge for the view, hike down to Neuschwanstein, and then catch the horse carriage from below the castle down to the parking lot (round-trip cost: €6.50). If you're on a tight schedule, consider taking the bus back down, as carriages can be unpredictable.

Neuschwanstein Castle

Dramatic Neuschwanstein is the castle that inspired Walt Disney. Despite being the one everyone visits, it's still a ▲▲▲ experience.

Castle Exterior

Imagine "Mad" King Ludwig as a boy, climbing the hills above his dad's castle, Hohenschwangau, dreaming up the ultimate fairy-tale castle. Inheriting the throne at the young age of 18, he had the power to make his dream concrete and stucco. Neuschwanstein (roughly "New Swanstone") was designed first by a theater-set designer...then by an architect. While it was built upon the ruins of an old castle and looks medieval, Neuschwanstein is modern iron-and-brick construction with a sandstone veneer—only about as old as the Eiffel Tower. It feels like something you'd see at a home show for 19th-century royalty. Built from 1869 to 1886, it's the epitome of the Romanticism popular in 19th-century Europe. Construction stopped with Ludwig's death (only a third of the interior was finished), and within six weeks, tourists were paying to go through it.

During World War II, the castle took on a sinister role. The Nazis used Neuschwanstein as one of their primary secret storehouses for stolen art. After the war, Allied authorities spent a year sorting through and redistributing the art, which filled 49 rail cars from this one location alone. It was the only time the unfinished rooms were put to use.

While you're waiting for your timed tour to pop up on the board,

Neuschwanstein Castle looks medieval but is only 150 years old and has modern conveniences.

climb the stairs to the upper courtyard to see more of the exterior, which isn't covered on your tour.

Inside the Castle—The Guided Visit

Once inside, your guide will herd you and up to 60 people through the castle, giving an interesting—yet often unenthusiastic and rushed—30-minute tour. You'll go up and down more than 300 steps (keep an eye out for a spiral staircase column that becomes a palm tree), visiting 15 lavish rooms with their original furnishings and fanciful wall paintings—mostly based on Wagnerian opera themes.

Ludwig's extravagant **throne room,** modeled in a Neo-Byzantine style, celebrates six valiant Christian kings (whose mantle Ludwig clearly believed he had donned) under a huge gilded-bronze, crown-like chandelier. The exquisite two-million-stone mosaic floor is a visual encyclopedia of animals and plants. While you're standing on a replica, original segments ring the perimeter. The most memorable stop may be the king's gilded-lily **bedroom,** with his elaborately carved canopy bed (with a forest of Gothic church spires on top), washstand (filled with water piped in from the Alps), and personal chapel. After passing through Ludwig's **living room** and a faux **grotto,** you'll climb to the fourth floor for the grand finale: the **Singers' Hall,** an ornately decorated space filled with murals depicting the story of Parzival, the legendary medieval knight with whom Ludwig identified.

After the Guided Tour—More Castle Exhibits

After the tour, weave through the crowded gift shop and past the WCs and café to see a 13-minute video (runs continuously) that tells the story of how the castle was built and illustrates all the unfinished parts of Ludwig's vision (more prickly towers, a central chapel, a fancy view terrace, an ornate bathhouse, and more). Finally, you'll see a digital model of Falkenstein—a whimsical, over-the-top, never-built castle that makes Neuschwanstein look stubby. Falkenstein occupied Ludwig's fantasies the year he died.

Then head downstairs to the kitchen (state-of-the-art for this high-tech king in its day), after which you'll come to a room containing a large castle model.

▸ *If you're ready to head **back to the village,** turn right to return on foot or take a horse-drawn carriage ride, or turn left to catch the bus (following signs toward Mary's Bridge).*

*Or, to **continue this tour,** adding about 40 minutes more to your visit, turn left to see Mary's Bridge (a 10-minute uphill hike) and then return to the village via the scenic Pöllat Gorge.*

▲▲Mary's Bridge (Marienbrücke)

The trail connecting Neuschwanstein to Mary's Bridge offers views back on Neuschwanstein's facade in one direction, and classic views of Hohenschwangau—perched on its little hill between lakes, with

Singers' Hall—murals tell a knight's tale

Ludwig's kitchen—state-of-the-art at the time

Mary's Bridge—dramatically spanning the Pöllat Gorge—has postcard views back toward the castle.

cut-glass peaks on the horizon—in the other. Climb up to Mary's Bridge (named for Ludwig's mom) to marvel at Ludwig's castle, just as Ludwig did. Jockey with a United Nations of tourists for the best angle—there's usually a line just to get onto the structure. This bridge was quite an engineering accomplishment 100 years ago.

▶ *If you enjoy romantic hikes, also plan to walk down through the...*

▲Pöllat Gorge (Pöllatschlucht)

The river gorge that slices into the rock just behind Neuschwanstein's lofty perch is an interesting and scenic alternative to shuffling down the crowded main road from the castle. While it takes an extra 15 minutes or so, it's well worth it. You'll find the trailhead just above the Neuschwanstein exit, on the path toward Mary's Bridge (look for *Pöllatschlucht* signs; trail closed in winter and sometimes impassable due to rockslides).

You'll begin by walking down a steep, well-maintained set of concrete stairs, with Germany's finest castle looming through the trees. Then you'll pop out along the river, passing a little beach (with neatly stacked stones) offering a view up at the grand waterfall that gushes beneath Mary's Bridge. From here, follow the river as it goes over

"Mad" King Ludwig (1845-1886)

A tragic figure, Ludwig II (a.k.a. "Mad" King Ludwig) ruled Bavaria for 22 years until his death in 1886 at the age of 40. Bavaria was weak. Politically, Ludwig's reality was to "rule" as either a pawn of Prussia or a pawn of Austria. Rather than deal with politics in Bavaria's capital, Munich, Ludwig frittered away most of his time at his family's hunting palace, Hohenschwangau. He spent much of his adult life constructing his fanciful Neuschwanstein Castle—like a kid builds a tree house—on a neighboring hill upon the scant ruins of a medieval castle. Here and in his other projects (such as Linderhof Castle and the never-built Falkenstein Castle), even as he strove to evoke medieval grandeur, he embraced the state-of-the-art technology of the Industrial Age in which he lived. Neuschwanstein had electricity, running water, and a telephone (but no Wi-Fi).

Ludwig was a true romantic living in a Romantic age. His best friends were artists, poets, and composers such as Richard Wagner. His palaces are wallpapered with misty medieval themes—especially those from Wagnerian operas.

Although Ludwig spent 17 years building Neuschwanstein, he lived in it only 172 days. Soon after he moved in (and before his vision for the castle was completed), Ludwig was declared mentally unfit to rule Bavaria and taken away. Two days after this eviction, Ludwig was found dead in a lake. To this day, people debate whether the king was murdered or committed suicide.

several smaller waterfalls—and stroll for a while along steel walkways and railings that make this slippery area safer. After passing an old wooden channel used to harness the power of all that water, you'll hit level ground; turn left and walk through a pleasantly untouristy residential settlement back toward the TI.

More Sights Near Neuschwanstein Castle

Outside of Neuschwanstein, the main sight to see is clearly Hohenschwangau Castle. The Tegelberg cable car and luge are a short bus, bike, or car ride (or 30-minute walk) away.

▲▲▲Hohenschwangau Castle

Standing quietly below Neuschwanstein, the big, yellow Hohenschwangau Castle is where Ludwig spent his summers as a young boy. Originally built in the 12th century, it was ruined by Napoleon. Ludwig's father, King Maximilian II, rebuilt it in 1830. Hohenschwangau (loosely translated as "High Swanland") was used by the royal family as a summer hunting lodge until 1912. The Wittelsbach family (which ruled Bavaria for nearly seven centuries) still owns the place (and lived in the annex—today's shop—until the 1970s).

The 45-minute guided tour gives a better glimpse of Ludwig's life than the more visited and famous Neuschwanstein Castle. Tours here are smaller (up to 35 people) and more relaxed.

The interior decor (mostly Neo-Gothic, like the castle itself) is harmonious, cohesive, and original—all done in 1835, with paintings inspired by Romantic themes. As you tour the castle, imagine how the paintings must have inspired young Ludwig. For 17 years, he lived here at his dad's place and followed the construction of his dream castle across the way—you'll see the telescope still set up and directed at Neuschwanstein.

You'll explore rooms on two floors—the queen's rooms, and then, upstairs, the king's. (Conveniently, their bedrooms were connected by a secret passage.) You'll see photos and busts of Ludwig and his little brother, Otto; some Turkish-style flourishes (to please the king, who had been impressed after a visit to the Orient); countless swans—try to find them (honoring the Knights of Schwangau, whose legacy the Wittelsbachs inherited); over-the-top gifts the Wittelsbachs received from their adoring subjects; and paintings of VIGs (very important Germans, including Martin Luther—who may or may not have visited here—and an infant Charlemagne).

One of the most impressive rooms is the Banquet Hall (also known as the Hall of Heroes); one vivid wall mural depicts a savage, yet bloodless, fifth-century barbarian battle. Just as the castle itself had running water and electricity despite its historic appearance

Hohenschwangau, Ludwig's boyhood home

There's winners and lugers, but fun for all.

(both were installed in the 1900s under King Luitpold, Ludwig's uncle), its Romantic decor presents a sanitized version of the medieval past, glossing over inconvenient details. You'll also see Ludwig's bedroom, which he inherited from his father. He kept most of the decor (including the nude nymphs frolicking over his bed) but painted the ceiling black and installed transparent stars that could be lit from the floor above to create the illusion of a night sky.

After the tour is over, wind through the castle gardens and imagine Ludwig frolicking here with his sights set on the hill far in the distance.

Museum of the Bavarian Kings
(Museum der Bayerischen Könige)
This modern, well-presented exhibit documents the history of the Wittelsbachs, Bavaria's former royal family. The museum is worthwhile only if you're captivated by this clan and have time to kill. (But trying to squeeze it between your two castle visits is rushing it—especially if you like to linger.)

▶ €14, includes audioguide and map; daily 9:00-17:00; no reservations required, mandatory lockers, Alpseestrasse 27, +49 8362 887 250, www.hohenschwangau.de.

▲Tegelberg Cable Car (Tegelbergbahn)
Just north of Neuschwanstein is a fun play zone around the mighty Tegelberg cable car, a scenic ride to the mountain's 5,500-foot summit. At the top on a clear day, you get great views of the Alps and Bavaria and the vicarious thrill of watching hang gliders and paragliders leap into airborne ecstasy. Weather permitting, scores of adventurous Germans

line up and leap from the launch ramp at the top of the lift. With someone leaving every two or three minutes, it's great for spectators. Thrill seekers with exceptional social skills may talk themselves into a tandem ride with a paraglider. From the top of Tegelberg, it's a steep and demanding 2.5-hour hike down to Ludwig's castle. (Avoid the treacherous trail directly below the cable car.) Around the cable car's valley station, you'll find a playground, a cheery eatery, the stubby remains of an ancient Roman villa, and a summer luge ride (described next).

▶ *€27 round-trip, €17.50 one-way; first ascent daily at 9:00; last descent April-Oct at 17:00, mid-Dec-March at 16:00, closed Nov-mid-Dec; 4/hour, 5-minute ride to the top, in bad weather call first to confirm, +49 8362 98360, www.tegelbergbahn.de.*

Getting There: From the castles, most #73 and #78 buses from Füssen continue to the Tegelbergbahn valley station (5-minute ride). It's a 30-minute walk or 10-minute bike ride from the castles.

▲Tegelberg Luge

Next to the cable car's valley station is a summer luge course (*Sommerrodelbahn*). A summer luge is like a bobsled on wheels. This course's stainless-steel track is heated, so it's often dry and open even when drizzly weather shuts down the concrete luges. A funky cable system pulls riders in their sleds to the top.

▶ *€5/ride, shareable 6-ride card—€20; typically open April-Sept daily 10:00-17:00 depending on weather, call first to confirm, waits can be long in good weather, no children under age 3, ages 3-7 may ride with an adult, +49 8362 98360, www.tegelbergbahn.de.*

FÜSSEN

The charming town of Füssen (FEW-sehn)—three miles west of Neuschwanstein—is the handiest overnight base for exploring the area. Dramatically situated under a renovated castle on the lively Lech River, it's historic and cobbled-cutesy. While Füssen is overrun by tourists in the summer, few venture to the back streets...which is where you'll find the real charm. It has some of the glitziest hotels in the area (as well as more affordable options) and some worthwhile sights. Everything I mention is walking distance in this small town, but renting a bike is a great way to get around.

Orientation to Füssen

Tourist Information: The TI is in a big yellow building in the center of town (Mon-Fri 9:00-17:00, Sat until 13:00, closed Sun; three blocks from station at Kaiser-Maximilian-Platz 1, +49 8362 93850, www.fuessen.de).

Arrival: The train station is three blocks from the center of town and the TI. Buses to Neuschwanstein, Reutte, and elsewhere leave from a parking lot next to the station. Drivers should be aware that Füssen is known for its traffic jams, and you can't drive into the Old Town. The most convenient lots (follow signs) are the underground P-5 (near the TI, €15/day) and the aboveground P-3 (off Kemptener Strasse, €14/day).

Hotel Card: Ask your hotel for a **Füssen Card,** which gives you free use of public transit in the immediate region (including the bus to Neuschwanstein and Wieskirche), as well as minor discounts at Neuschwanstein, Hohenschwangau, Museum of the Bavarian Kings, and several other attractions. Be sure to return the card before you leave town. After the hotel activates the card, it can take an hour or two before it works at sights and on buses.

Bike Rental: Ski Sport Luggi has good bikes and tips for the area (prices per 24 hours: €15-city bike, €20-mountain bike, €30-electric bike; Tue-Fri 9:00-12:00 & 14:00-17:30, Sat until 13:00, closed Sun-Mon; shorter hours off-season, call ahead to reserve, ID required, Luitpoldstrasse 11, +49 8362 505 9155, www.ski-sport-luggi.de).

Car Rental: Hertz Rental Car is an easy taxi ride from the center (Mon-Fri 8:00-12:00 & 14:00-18:00, Sat 8:00-12:00, closed Sun and holidays, Füssener Strasse 112, +49 8362 986 580, www.hertz.de).

Sights in and near Füssen

Füssen Heritage Museum

The town's one must-see sight stars *Dance of Death*. Painted shortly after the devastating 1590 plague, it shows 20 people from different social classes, each dancing with the Grim Reaper. The museum also has some exquisitely decorated Baroque rooms, plus exhibits on violin making and Füssen's other important trades.

▶ *€6, Tue-Sun 11:00-17:00, closed Mon; shorter hours and closed Mon-Thu Nov-March; +49 8362 903 143, www.museum.fuessen.de.*

▲Royal Crystal Baths (Königliche Kristall-Therme)

A mile east of town is this pool/sauna complex—the perfect way to re-lax on a rainy day or to cool off on a hot one. It has two heated indoor pools and a café in the main complex; a shallow kiddie pool, a lap pool, a heated *Kristallbad* with massage jets and a whirlpool, and a salty mineral bath outside; and extensive saunas upstairs (if you're OK with nudity). From Füssen, drive, take the bus (#73 or #78, ask driver for best stop), bike, or walk (30 minutes) across the river, turn left toward Schwangau, and then, about a mile later, turn left at signs for *Kristall-Therme*. It's at Am Ehberg 16.

▶ *Baths only—€15.50/2 hours, €23/4 hours, €29.50/all day; saunas—€7 ex-tra, towel rental-€3, bathrobe rental-€5, bathing suits sold but not rent-ed; Sun-Thu 9:00-21:00, Fri-Sat until 22:00; nude swimming everywhere Tue after 19:00; +49 8362 926 940, www.kristalltherme-schwangau.de.*

Bike and Boat Rides

On a beautiful day, nothing beats a **bike ride** around the bright-tur-quoise Forggensee, a nearby lake. This 20-mile loop is exclusively on bike paths (give it a half-day; it's tight to squeeze it into the afternoon after a morning of castle visits, but possible with an early start). Locals swear that going clockwise is less work, but either way has a couple of strenuous uphill parts (total elevation gain of about 600 feet). Rent a bike (ideally a 21-speed), pack a picnic lunch, and figure about a three-hour round-trip. From Füssen, follow *Festspielhaus* signs; once you reach the theater, follow *Forggensee Rundweg* signs.

You can also take a **boat ride** on the Forggensee, leaving either from the Füssen "harbor" (*Bootshafen*) or the theater (*Festspielhaus*), a 25-minute walk north of town (€12/50-minute cruise, 5/day; €16/2-hour cruise, 3/day; runs daily June-mid-Oct, no boats off-season, +49 8362 921 363, www.stadt-fuessen.de). Unless it's very crowded in the summer, you can bring your bike onto the boat and get off across the lake—shortening the total loop.

Lech Falls and Treetop Walkway (Baumkronenweg Ziegelwies)

Another pleasant walk from town is to head south across the river and turn right (upstream) to Lech Falls, a thunderous waterfall.

Just past the falls on the road to Reutte (across the border in Austria), an elevated wooden "treetop path" lets you stroll for a third of a mile, high in the trees on a graceful yet sturdy suspension-bridge-like

Füssen has plenty of hotels, eateries, and charm.

Lech Falls, a short walk from town

structure 60 feet in the air. The walkway crosses the Austria-Germany border and offers views of the surrounding mountains and the "wild" alpine Lech River, which can be a smooth glacier-blue mirror one day and a muddy torrent the next. The Austrian end (closer to Reutte) has a large parking lot and a tiny ticket booth. At the German end (closer to Füssen) there is a nature center and café, and parking is scarce.

▶ €5, free for kids 15 and under, daily 9:00-19:30, April and mid-Oct-Nov 10:00-16:00, closed Dec-March and in bad weather, Tiroler Strasse 10, +49 8362 9002 2150, www.baumkronenweg.eu.

Sleeping and Eating in Füssen

My recommendations are within a few handy blocks of the train station and the town center. Many hotels give a 5-10 percent discount for two-night stays—always ask.

Sleeping: A few big fancy hotels are within a few minutes' walk of the train station, including the **$$$ Hotel Schlosskrone** (Prinzregentenplatz 2, +49 8362 930 180, www.schlosskrone.de) and **$$$ Hotel Hirsch** (Kaiser-Maximilian-Platz 7, +49 8362 93980, www.hotelfuessen.de).

These smaller, mid-priced hotels are also centrally located: **$$ Altstadthotel zum Hechten** (Ritterstrasse 6, +49 8362 91600, www.hotel-hechten.com) and **$ Gästehaus Schöberl** (Luitpoldstrasse 14, +49 8362 922 411, www.schoeberl-fuessen.de).

For budget beds, consider **¢ Old Kings Design Hostel** (dorm rooms and three private doubles, Franziskanergasse 2, +49 8362 883 4090, www.oldkingshostel.com).

Eating: $$ Restaurant Ritterstub'n offers delicious German grub, salads, veggie plates, and a fun kids' menu; eat inside or in the courtyard (Tue-Sun 11:30-14:00 & 17:30-21:30, closed Mon, Ritterstrasse 4, +49 8362 7759). **$$ Schenke & Wirtshaus** dishes up traditional Bavarian dishes and pike (*Hecht*) pulled from the Lech River (daily 11:30-21:00, Ritterstrasse 6, +49 8362 91600). **$$$ Ristorante La Perla** is a lively Italian restaurant with a sleek interior and quiet streetside tables (Tue-Sun 11:30-21:30, closed Mon, Drehergasse 44, +49 8362 7155).

For simpler fare, **$ Thuy Golden Stäbchen** serves a mix of Vietnamese, Chinese, and Thai food with outdoor tables and a castle view (daily 10:00-22:00, Hinteregasse 29, +49 8362 939 7714). For groceries and picnic supplies, try the discount **Netto** supermarket, at the roundabout across from Hotel Schlosskrone, or the midrange **REWE** in the Theresienhof shopping complex (both supermarkets open Mon-Sat 7:00-20:00, closed Sun).

MORE BAVARIAN SIGHTS

There are many more great Bavarian sights, but most are best with a rental car.

There's the ▲▲ **Wieskirche,** an ornately decorated Baroque church in a humble pasture (www.wieskirche.de). ▲ **Oberammergau** is Germany's woodcarving capital and home of the famous Passion Play (www.ammergauer-alpen.de). **Ettal Monastery** is another fancy church (www.klosterettal.de). ▲▲ **Linderhof,** yet another of Ludwig's castles, is an exquisite mini-Versailles with a palace and gardens set in the woods (www.linderhof.de). For more in-depth coverage on all these sights, buy my *Rick Steves Germany* guidebook.

With a car, you could see all of these (as well as Neuschwanstein) in a single long day from either Munich or Füssen. Or, with a lot of patience, you could reach the Wieskirche and Oberammergau by bus from Füssen—get details at the Füssen TI or at Bahn.com.

Salzburg, Austria

Salzburg, just over the Austrian border, makes a fun day trip from Munich (1.5 hours by direct train). It has a charmingly preserved Old Town, a dramatic natural setting, Baroque churches, and one of Europe's largest medieval fortresses—Hohensalzburg. It's a musical mecca for fans of hometown-boy Mozart, the movie *The Sound of Music,* and classical-music concerts. Despite the tourist crowds, it's a city with style.

Salzburg is steeped in history. For centuries, it was an independent city-state, ruled by a prince-archbishop. Today you can visit his hilltop fortress, his luxurious Residenz, or his fountain-spewing summer palace, Hellbrunn. This chapter focuses on seeing Salzburg as a day trip, but it also makes a great overnight stay, so I've recommended some hotels and restaurants.

ORIENTATION TO SALZBURG

Getting There: Trains from Munich to Salzburg (and vice versa) run about twice per hour from early morning until midnight. It costs about €50 round-trip and takes 1.5 hours (2 hours on slower trains). The economical Bayern-Ticket day pass for Bavaria works for Salzburg (see page 122). In fact, all rail passes that include Germany also include Salzburg (which is considered a border town). Salzburg's train station has a TI, luggage lockers, and a handy Spar supermarket.

Getting to the Old Town: Getting downtown from the station is a snap. Simply step outside, find bus platform C (labeled *Zentrum-Altstadt*), and buy a ticket from the machine (€2.20 *Stundenkarte*). Buses #1, #3, #5, and #6 all do the same route into the city center before diverging. Bus #25 (from platform B) follows the same path to the center and continues to Hellbrunn Palace. For most sights and Old Town hotels, get off just after the bridge (either Rathaus or Hanuschplatz, depending on the bus). A taxi from the station to most hotels is about €8.

Tourist Information: Salzburg's TI (+43 662 889 870, www.salzburg. info) has two helpful branches: at the train station (daily 9:00-17:00, until 18:00 in summer) and on Mozartplatz in the old center (daily 9:00-18:00, July-Aug often until 19:00, closed Sun in winter).

Salzburg Card: Hotels and TIs sell the Salzburg Card, which covers all public transportation (including the Mönchsberg elevator and funicular to the fortress) and admission to all the city sights (including Hellbrunn Palace and a river cruise). As Salzburg's sights are pricey, the card can be a money saver, and it's also a convenience. The card makes financial sense if you'll be seeing two major sights on a single day, or three sights over two days. You can also buy the card online (€30/24 hours, €39/48 hours, €45/72 hours, www.salzburg.info).

Walking Tours: You can take a one-hour, informative guided walk of the Old Town without a reservation any day—just show up at the TI on Mozartplatz at the tour time and pay the guide (€10, daily at 12:15 and sometimes at 14:00, +43 664 340 1757, Frau Schneeweiss).

Salzburg at a Glance

▲▲▲**Salzburg Town Walk** Old Town's best sights in a handy orientation walk. See page 144.

▲▲**Salzburg Cathedral** Glorious, harmonious Baroque main church of Salzburg. **Hours:** Mon-Sat 9:00-18:00, Sun from 13:00. See page 147.

▲▲*The Sound of Music* **Tours** Bus or bike through S.O.M. sights of Salzburg and surrounding countryside. See page 163.

▲▲**Getreidegasse** Picturesque old shopping lane with characteristic wrought-iron signs. See page 156.

▲▲**Salzburg Museum** Best place for city history. **Hours:** Tue-Sun 9:00-17:00, closed Mon. See page 157.

▲▲**Mozart's Birthplace** House where Mozart was born in 1756, featuring his instruments and other exhibits. **Hours:** Daily July-Aug 8:30-19:30, Sept-June 9:00-17:30. See page 158.

▲▲**Hohensalzburg Fortress** Imposing mountaintop castle, with small museums, commanding views, and concerts most evenings. **Hours:** Museums open daily 8:30-20:00, Oct-April 9:30-17:00. See page 160.

▲▲**Hellbrunn Palace** Lavish palace on the outskirts of town featuring gardens with trick fountains. **Hours:** Daily 9:00-17:30, July-Aug until 18:00, April and Oct until 16:30, closed Nov-March. See page 162.

▲**DomQuartier Museums** Prince-Archbishop Wolf Dietrich's Residenz palace, cathedral viewpoint, and religious art. **Hours:** Wed-Mon 10:00-17:00, closed Tue. See page 157.

For private guides, I recommend **Gertraud Kamml** (€170/3 hours, €220/4 hours, +43 664 352 6329, www.kunstschreibwerkstatt. com), **Sabine Rath** (€175/2 hours, €260/4 hours, +43 664 201 6492, www.tourguide-salzburg.com), or **Anna Stellnberger** (€160/2 hours, €240/4 hours, +43 664 787 5177, anna.stellnberger@aon.at).

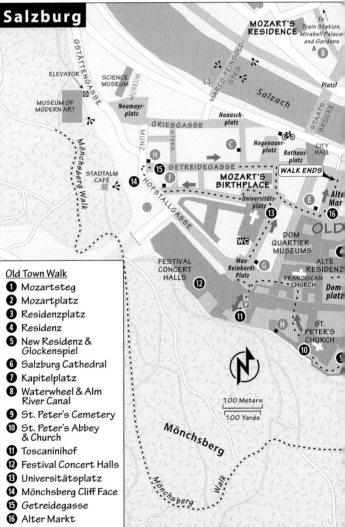

Salzburg

Old Town Walk

1 Mozartsteg
2 Mozartplatz
3 Residenzplatz
4 Residenz
5 New Residenz & Glockenspiel
6 Salzburg Cathedral
7 Kapitelplatz
8 Waterwheel & Alm River Canal
9 St. Peter's Cemetery
10 St. Peter's Abbey & Church
11 Toscaninihof
12 Festival Concert Halls
13 Universitätsplatz
14 Mönchsberg Cliff Face
15 Getreidegasse
16 Alter Markt

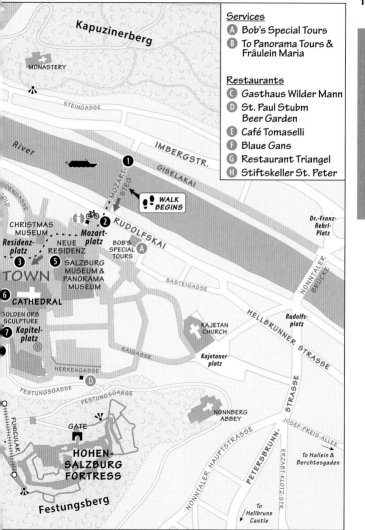

SALZBURG TOWN WALK

Salzburg, a city of 150,000 (Austria's fourth-largest), is split in two by the Salzach River. North of the river lies the New Town (Neustadt), with the train station and a few sights.

But our walk focuses on the Old Town (Altstadt). Nestled between the Salzach River and Salzburg's little Mönchsberg mountain, this neighborhood holds nearly all the charm and most of the tourists. Allow about two hours.

🎧 Download my free Salzburg Town Walk audio tour.

▶ *Begin at the Mozartsteg, the wrought-iron, Art Nouveau pedestrian bridge built in 1903 over the Salzach River.*

❶ Mozartsteg

Take in the charming, well-preserved, historic core of Salzburg's Old Town. The skyline bristles with Baroque steeples and green copper domes. Salzburg has 38 Catholic churches, plus two Protestant churches and a synagogue. The biggest green dome is the cathedral, which we'll visit shortly. Overlooking it all is the castle called Hohensalzburg Fortress—beefed up with the threats that came with the Thirty Years' War in the 17th century.

The Salzach is called "salt river" not because it's salty, but because of the precious cargo it once carried. The salt mines of Hallein are 12 miles upstream. For 2,000 years, barges carried salt from here to the wider world—to the Danube, the Black Sea, and on to the Mediterranean. As barges passed through, they had to pay a toll on their salt. The city was made great from the trading of salt (*Salz*) defended by a castle (*Burg*)—"Salz-burg."

Start your Salzburg walk at the river.

Mozart statue on Mozartplatz

▶ *From the bridge, walk one block toward the hill-capping castle into the Old Town. Pass the traffic barriers and turn right into a big square, called...*

❷ Mozartplatz

This square is named for the man honored by the central statue—Wolfgang Amadeus Mozart. The great composer was born a few blocks from here and spent most of his first 25 years (1756-1781) in Salzburg. He and his father both served Salzburg's rulers before Wolfgang went on to seek his fortune in Vienna. The statue (considered a poor likeness) was erected in 1842, just after the 50th anniversary of Mozart's death. This date could be considered the start of the cult of Mozart, as a group of enthusiasts (including his widow, Constanze) founded the Salzburg Mozarteum Foundation at about that time, with a mission to popularize and perform his music. A music festival in 1856, on the 100th anniversary of Mozart's birth, planted the seed for what would become the world-renowned Salzburg Festival. Soon, Salzburg would be a stop on the romantic Grand Tour of Europe.

Mozart stands atop the spot where the first Salzburgers settled. Two thousand years ago, the Romans had a salt-trading town here called Juvavum. In the year 800, Salzburg—by then Christian and home to an important abbey—joined Charlemagne's Holy Roman Empire as an independent city. The first market was on this square and the city developed from here. The Church of St. Michael (whose pastel tower overlooks the square) dates from that time. It's Salzburg's oldest, if not biggest, parish church.

▶ *Note the TI, then walk toward the cathedral and into the big square with the huge fountain.*

❸ Residenzplatz

As Salzburg's governing center, this square has long been ringed with important buildings. The cathedral dominates. The Residenz—the former palace of Salzburg's rulers—is to the right (as you face the cathedral). To the left is the New Residenz, with its bell tower.

In the 1600s, this square got a makeover in the then-fashionable Italian Baroque style. The rebuilding started under energetic Prince-Archbishop Wolf Dietrich, who ruled from 1587 to 1612. Dietrich had been raised in Rome. He counted the Medicis as his cousins and had grandiose Italian ambitions for Salzburg. Conveniently for him, the existing cathedral burned down in 1598. Dietrich set about rebuilding it as part of his grand vision to make Salzburg the "Rome of the North."

The fountain is as Italian as can be, an over-the-top version of Bernini's famous Triton Fountain in Rome. Triton, on top, blows his conch-shell horn as water cascades down the basins and sprays playfully in the wind.

Notice that Salzburg's buildings are made from three distinctly different types of stone. Most common is the chunky gray conglomerate rock (like the cathedral's side walls) quarried from the nearby cliffs. There's also white marble (like the cathedral's towers and windows) and red marble (best seen in monuments inside buildings), both from the Alps near Berchtesgaden.

▶ *Turn your attention to the building on the right, the...*

❹ Residenz

This was the palace of Salzburg's powerful ruler, the prince-archbishop—a ruler with both the political powers of a prince and the religious authority of an archbishop. The ornate Baroque entrance (with the

The Residenz, opulent home of Salzburg's former prince-archbishop

prince-archbishop's proud coat of arms) attests to the connections these rulers had with Rome. You can step inside the Residenz courtyard to get a glimpse of the impressive digs (to see the fancy interior, you must buy a DomQuartier ticket—see listing later, under "More Sights in Salzburg").

▶ *At the opposite end of Residenzplatz from the Residenz is the...*

❺ New (Neue) Residenz

In the days of the prince-archbishops, this building hosted parties in its lavish rooms. Today, the New Residenz houses both the Salzburg Museum and the Panorama Museum (see "More Sights in Salzburg").

The New Residenz bell tower has a hard-working **glockenspiel**. This 18th-century carillon has 35 bells and chimes daily at 7:00, 11:00, and 18:00.

▶ *Exit the square by walking under the prince-archbishop's skyway. You'll step into Domplatz (Cathedral Square). For a good place to view the cathedral facade, walk to the far end of the square.*

❻ Salzburg Cathedral (Salzburger Dom)

Salzburg's cathedral was one of the first Italian Baroque buildings north of the Alps, built thanks to a 10 percent tax on all salt traded here. The dome stands 230 feet high, and two domed towers flank the very Italianesque entrance.

The church was consecrated in 1628. The cathedral was the center of power for the prince-archbishop in his religious role, and the government buildings surrounding it served his needs as a secular prince.

Before entering the cathedral, step back to admire the facade. Notice the play on perspective that occurs when you line up the statue of Mary (in the center of the square) with the two angels (on the center of the facade): They can be seen as crowning her as the queen of heaven. Read the facade like a Bible of stone: Jesus is on top, Moses and Elijah—representing the Old Testament—are next. Below that are the four evangelists (Matthew, Mark, Luke, and John), and at the bottom are the fathers of the Salzburg church mixing it up with the fathers of St. Peter's Basilica in Rome (left to right): St. Rupert (with his salt cask), Peter (with his keys), Paul (with his sword), and St. Virgil (with a model of Salzburg's first cathedral from 774).

An Italian Baroque fountain by the Baroque towers of the Cathedral—"The Rome of the North"

The statue of Mary in front of Salzburg Cathedral being "crowned" by angels on the facade

As you approach the church, pause at the **iron gates.** The dates on the doors are milestones in the church's history. In the year 774, the first church, built in Romanesque style, was consecrated by St. Virgil, an Irish monk who became Salzburg's bishop. It was destroyed by fire in 1167, rebuilt, and then burned again in 1598. It was replaced in 1628 by the one you see today. The year 1959 marks the completion of repairs after a WWII bomb severely damaged the dome.

Now enter the church (€5, Mon-Sat 9:00-18:00, Sun from 13:00, audioguide-€3, www.salzburger-dom.at). Because it was built in just 14 years (from 1614 to 1628), the church boasts an unusually harmonious Baroque architecture. And it's big—330 feet long, 230 feet tall—built with sturdy pillars and broad arches. When Pope John Paul II visited in 1998, some 5,000 people packed the place.

Under the soaring dome, look up and admire the exceptional stucco work, by an artist from Milan. It's molded into elaborate garlands, angels, and picture frames, some of it brightly painted. You're surrounded by the tombs (and portraits) of 10 archbishops.

You're also surrounded by four organs. (Actually, five—counting

The Cathedral Mass has world-class music.

Modern art in this cultured city

the biggest organ, over the entrance.) Mozart served as organist here for two years, and he composed several Masses that are still played today. Salzburg's prince-archbishops were great patrons of music, with a personal orchestra that played religious music in the cathedral and dinner music in the Residenz. The tradition of music continues today. Sunday Mass here can be a musical spectacle—with all five organs playing and balconies filled with singers and musicians, creating glorious surround-sound. Think of the altar in Baroque terms, as the center of a stage, with sunrays serving as spotlights in this dramatic and sacred theater.

In the left transept, descend the stairs into the crypt (and the 8th-century street level). Here, among the remains of the Romanesque cathedral that preceded today's church, is the resting place of centuries of archbishops and prince-archbishops.

Work your way back to the entrance via the left aisle. In the chapel in the far corner find a dark bronze baptismal font. It dates from 1320—a rare survivor from the medieval-era cathedral (the lid is from 1959). In 1756, little Wolfgang Amadeus Mozart was baptized here. For the next 25 years, this would be his home church.

▶ *As you leave the cathedral, turn left, heading toward the distant fortress on the hill. You'll soon reach a spacious square with a golden orb.*

❼ Kapitelplatz

The playful modern sculpture of a man atop a golden orb is part of Salzburg's Walk of Modern Art. Follow the orb-man's gaze up the hill to **Hohensalzburg Fortress.** Construction of the fortress began in 1077. Salzburg made it powerful in hopes of not getting caught up in struggles between the German Holy Roman Emperor and the pope. Over the centuries, the small castle grew into a mighty, whitewashed fortress—so impressive that no army even tried attacking for over 800 years. These days, you can tour the castle grounds, visit some interior rooms and museums, and enjoy incredible views (see listing later, under "More Sights in Salzburg"). The castle's earliest funicular dates back to the 1500s, when animals pulled cargo up its tracks; today's funicular is electric, from 1910.

Now walk across the square to the pond surrounded by a balustrade and adorned with a Trevi-fountain-like **statue of Neptune.** The god of the sea rides his seahorse, flanked by tritons. The pond was built as an 18th-century horse-and-buggy wash—like an old-time car wash. Notice the gold lettering above Neptune. It reads, "Leopold the Prince Built Me." But the artist added a clever twist. The inscription uses the letters "LLDVI," and so on. Those are also Roman numerals—add 'em up: L is 50, D is 500, and so on. It all adds up to 1732—the year the pond was built.

This square hosts many free events and concerts (including videos of great Salzburg Festival performances on a jumbo screen).

▶ *With your back to the cathedral, leave the square, exiting through the gate in the far-right corner.*

❽ Waterwheel (Wasserrad) and the Alm River Canal (Almkanal)

The waterwheel is part of a clever, still-functioning canal system built in the 12th century to bring water to Salzburg from the foothills of the Alps, 10 miles away in Bavaria. The rushing water was harnessed to waterwheels, which powered mills. This particular waterwheel (actually, it's a modern replacement) once ground grain into flour to make bread for the monks of St. Peter's Abbey. Nowadays, you can pop into the adjacent **bakery** and buy a fresh-baked roll for about a euro.

▶ *You've entered the borders of the former St. Peter's Abbey, a monastic complex of churches, courtyards, businesses (like the bakery), and a cemetery. Find the* Katakomben *sign and step through the wrought-iron gates into a lovely cemetery (free, open daily, silence requested).*

❾ St. Peter's Cemetery (Petersfriedhof)

This collection of lovingly tended graves abuts the sheer rock face of

Waterwheel of the former abbey

Graves and churches of St. Peter's Cemetery

the Mönchsberg. Tended by descendants of the deceased, today St. Peter's Cemetery is calm and filled with love as families visit and little memory gardens blossom with seasonal flowers.

In Austria, gravesites are rented, not owned. Rent bills are sent out every 10 years. If no one cares enough to make the payment, your tombstone is removed.

Walk in about 50 yards past the well to a junction of lanes in the middle of the cemetery. You're surrounded by three churches, each founded in the early Middle Ages atop a pagan Celtic holy site. The biggest church, St. Peter's, sticking its big Romanesque apse into the cemetery, is our next stop.

The cemetery played a role in *The Sound of Music*. In the movie, this was where the Von Trapp family hid behind tombstones from the Nazis. (The scene was actually filmed on a Hollywood set inspired by St. Peter's Cemetery.)

Look up the cliff, which has a few buildings attached—called (not quite accurately) "catacombs." Legendary hermit-monks are said to have lived in the hillside here 1,500 years ago. For a small fee, you can enter the *Katakomben* and climb lots of steps to see a few old caves, a chapel, and some fine city views (entrance at the base of the cliff, under the arcade—look for #LIV over the arch; €2, visit takes 10 minutes; daily 10:00-12:30 & 13:00-18:00, Oct-April until 17:00).

Explore the arcade at the base of the cliff with its various burial chapels. Alcove #XXI has the tomb of the cathedral architect Santino Solari—forever facing his creation. At the catacombs entry (#LIV) are two interesting tombs marked by plaques on the floor. "Marianne" is Mozart's sister, nicknamed "Nannerl." Michael Haydn was the brother of Joseph Haydn. He succeeded Mozart as church cathedral organist.

▶ *Exit the cemetery through the green door at the opposite end. Just outside, you enter a large courtyard anchored by...*

⑩ St. Peter's Abbey and Church

You're standing at the birthplace of Christianity in Salzburg. St. Peter's Abbey—the monastery that surrounds this courtyard—was founded in 696, barely two centuries after the fall of Rome. About 20 monks and their abbot still pray and work (*ora et labora*) here as Benedictines have for over a millennium (free, daily 8:00-21:00, Nov-March until 19:00, www.stift-stpeter.at).

The St. Peter Stiftskulinarium restaurant on the left (known these days for its Mozart Dinner Concert) brags that Charlemagne ate here in the year 803, making it (perhaps) the oldest restaurant in Europe. Opposite the restaurant is the monastery shop with monk-made gifts from around Austria (Klosterladen St. Peter, open 10:00-18:00, closed Sun).

St. Peter's Church dates from 1147. As you enter, pause in the atrium to admire the Romanesque **tympanum** (from 1250) over the inner doorway. Jesus sits on a rainbow, flanked by Peter and Paul. Beneath them is a stylized Tree of Life, and overhead, a Latin inscription reading, "I am the door to life, and only through me can you find eternal life."

Entering the **nave,** you can understand why this is a popular wedding church in Salzburg. It's Salzburg's only Rococo interior—all whitewashed, with highlights of pastel green, gold, and red. In the 18th century, the roof was raised and clear windows added for light.

The ceiling paintings feature St. Peter receiving the keys from Christ (center painting), walking on water, and joining the angels in heaven.

The monastery was founded by **St. Rupert** (c. 650-718). Find his statue at the main altar—he's the second gold statue from the left. Rupert arrived as a Christian missionary in what was then a largely pagan land. He preached the gospel, reopened the Roman salt mines, and established the city. It was he who named it "Salzburg." **Rupert's tomb** is midway up the right aisle.

▶ *Leave the abbey square opposite where you entered. You'll walk*

Christ presides over the church entrance at St. Peter's Abbey, where Christian Salzburg began.

through a similar second square with architectural features from the 1920s. Passing through that square you reach...

⑪ Toscaninihof

In this small courtyard, you get a peek at the back end of the large Festival Hall complex. The Festival Hall has three theaters and seats 5,000 people (see photo on the wall).

The tunnel leads to the actual concert hall. It's generally closed, but you may be able to look through nearby doorways and see carpenters building stage sets or hear performers practicing for an upcoming show.

The Von Trapp family performed here in the Festival Hall. In the movie, this backstage courtyard is where Captain von Trapp nervously waited before walking onstage to sing "Edelweiss." Then the family slipped away to begin their escape from the Nazis.

This square is named for Arturo Toscanini, who was musical director of the Salzburg Festival in the 1930s. He fled to New York in

1937, the year before the Von Trapp family escaped (Toscanini had an easier time).

▶ *From here, we'll head across Max-Reinhardt-Platz. But first look to your left, toward the Festival District, with the concert halls that host the annual summer music event.*

⑫ Festival Concert Halls

The Salzburg Festival was started in the austere 1920s, after World War I. As Salzburg couldn't afford a new concert hall, they remodeled what were once the prince-archbishop's stables and riding school into music venues. You can still see the arched features of the original riding-school building.

▶ *Continue straight along the right side of the big church, passing the recommended Restaurant Triangel, popular sausage stands, and a public WC, then enter...*

⑬ Universitätsplatz

This square, home to the huge Baroque Kollegienkirche (University Church), also hosts Salzburg's liveliest open-air produce market (and a lot of touristy food stands). It's at its best early Saturday morning, when the farmers are in town. The fancy yellow facade overlooking the square marks the back end of Mozart's Birthplace, which we'll see (from the other side) shortly.

Find the fountain at the far end of the market (it's about 50 yards past the church). As with public marketplaces elsewhere, it's for washing fruit and vegetables. This fountain—though modern in design—is still part of a medieval-era water system. The water plummets down a hole and on to the river. The sundial over the water hole shows both the time and the date.

▶ *Continue toward the end of the square. Along the way, you'll pass several nicely arcaded medieval passageways (on the right), which lead to Salzburg's old main street, Getreidegasse—where we'll end this tour shortly. When you reach the traffic-control bollards, you're looking at the...*

⑭ Mönchsberg Cliff Face

Rising some 1,700 feet above you is the Mönchsberg, Salzburg's mountain. It served as a quarry for the city's 17th-century growth spurt—the bulk of the cathedral, for example, is built of this conglomerate rock.

Walk to the base of the cliff, where you'll see what was the giant horse trough for the stables of the prince-archbishops. Paintings show the various breeds and temperaments of horses in the stable. Like Vienna, Salzburg had a passion for the equestrian arts.

▶ *Walk a block toward the river. Opposite the church, turn right onto the long pedestrian street called...*

⑮ Getreidegasse

Old Salzburg's colorful main drag, Getreidegasse has been a center of trade since Roman times. Check out all the old wrought-iron signs that advertise what's sold inside. There are signs advertising spirits, a book maker, and a horn indicating a place for the postal coach. A brewery has a star for the name of the beer, "Sternbräu." There's a window maker, a key maker, a pastry shop, a tailor, a pretzel maker, a pharmacy, a hat maker, and...ye olde hamburger shoppe, McDonald's.

Sample homemade spirits at Sporer (#39) or ice cream at Eisgrotte (#40). Across from Eisgrotte, a tunnel leads to Balkan Grill (sign reads *Bosna Grill*), the local choice for the very best wurst in town. At #28 (a blacksmith shop since the 1400s), Herr Wieber welcomes the curious.

At Getreidegasse #9, the knot of excited tourists marks the childhood home of Salzburg's most famous resident—Mozart.

▶ *At Getreidegasse #3, turn right, into the passageway. When you reach the time-capsule café **Schatz Konditorei** (worth a stop for a pastry), turn left through the passage. When you reach Sigmund-Haffner-Gasse, glance to the left (for a nice view of the City Hall tower), then*

Upscale horse trough by the Mönchsberg   Getreidegasse—each shop has an ID sign

turn right. Walk along Sigmund-Haffner-Gasse and take your first left to reach a square called…

⑯ Alter Markt

This is Salzburg's old marketplace. Here you'll find a sausage stand, a fine old chocolate shop, and the venerable (and recommended) Café Tomaselli.

▶ *Our walk is over. If you're up for more sightseeing, you're right in the center of it all. Read on.*

MORE SIGHTS IN SALZBURG

The best Old Town sights are linked in my self-guided walk, earlier. I've covered some of those sights in more detail next. I've also listed a few other sightseeing options—if you have extra time.

In the Old Town

▲DomQuartier Museums (including the Residenz)

The interconnected museums of the DomQuartier, ringing the Domplatz, focus on religious art and the history of Salzburg's prince-archbishops. Your DomQuartier ticket admits you to a circular, indoor route through the Residenz (the ornate former palace), the cathedral, and a couple of adjoining buildings. You'll see lavish apartments, a fine collection of paintings, and enjoy the chance to walk across the gallery to the organ loft and peer into the cavernous cathedral.

▶ *€13, includes good audioguide, Wed-Mon 10:00-17:00, closed Tue, last entry one hour before closing, Residenzplatz 1, +43 662 8042 2109, www.domquartier.at.*

▲▲Salzburg Museum and ▲Panorama Museum

This is your best look at the art and cultural history of Salzburg, displayed in lavish rooms where Salzburg's rulers entertained. The permanent exhibit called "The Salzburg Myth" tells how the town's physical beauty attracted 19th-century Romantics, making it one of Europe's first tourist destinations. A side room hosts a celebration of Salzburg's music scene, with interactive exhibits, musical instruments, and audio samples, showing how the arrival of the music festival in the 1920s spurred Salzburg's status still more. Next comes the glory days of the prince-archbishops (1500-1800), with their portraits displayed in impressive ceremonial rooms. Room 2.11—a big, colorful hall—showcases the most famous prince-archbishop, Wolf Dietrich von Raitenau, the Renaissance Man who largely created the city we see today.

From the Salzburg Museum entryway, find the underground "Panorama Passage" that leads to the New Residence, where the Panorama Museum displays a wrap-around painting of the city, giving a 360-degree look at Salzburg in the year 1829.

▶ *Salzburg Museum—€9, €10 combo-ticket with Panorama Museum, includes multimedia guide, Tue-Sun 9:00-17:00, closed Mon, café, on Residenzplatz, +43 662 620 8080, www.salzburgmuseum.at. Panorama Museum—€4.50, daily 9:00-17:00, +43 662 620 808 730.*

▲▲Mozart's Birthplace (Geburtshaus)

In 1747, Leopold Mozart—a musician in the prince-archbishop's band—moved into this small rental unit with his new bride. Soon they had a baby girl (Nannerl), and in 1756, a little boy was born—Wolfgang

Mozart learned to play piano and violin in this 18th-century apartment.

Mozart's Salzburg

Salzburg was Mozart's home for the first 25 years of his brief, 35-year life. He was born on Getreidegasse and baptized in the cathedral. He played his first big concert, at age six, at the Residenz. He was the organist for the cathedral, conducted the prince-archbishop's orchestra, and dined at (what's now called) Café Tomaselli. It was from Salzburg that he gained Europe-wide fame, touring the continent with his talented performing family. At age 17, Mozart and his family moved into lavish digs at (today's) Mozart's Residence.

As his fame and ambitions grew, Mozart eventually left Salzburg to pursue his dreams in Vienna. His departure from Salzburg's royal court in 1781 is the stuff of legend. Mozart, full of himself, announced that he was quitting. The prince-archbishop essentially said, "You can't quit; you're fired!" and as Mozart walked out, he was literally kicked in the ass.

Amadeus Mozart. It was here that Mozart learned to play piano and violin, and composed his first boy-genius works. Even after the family gained fame, touring Europe's palaces and becoming the toast of Salzburg, they continued living in this rather cramped, typical 18th-century apartment until 1773, when they finally moved to bigger digs across the river.

Today this is the most popular Mozart sight in town—for fans, it's almost a pilgrimage. Shuffling through with the crowds, you'll peruse three floors of rooms displaying paintings, letters, personal items, and lots of context, all bringing life to the Mozart story.

▶ *€12, €18.50 combo-ticket with Mozart's Residence; daily July-Aug 8:30-19:30, Sept-June 9:00-17:30; Getreidegasse 9, +43 662 844 313, www.mozarteum.at. Avoid crowds by visiting early or late.*

Atop the Cliffs Above the Old Town

There are three ways to get up to the cliffs: The **climb** up or down is steep but quick. Paths or stairs lead up from the Augustiner Bräustübl beer hall/garden, Toscaninihof (near the Salzburg Festival concert halls), and Festungsgasse (at the base of the fortress). The elevator is next to the Museum of Modern Art entry and puts you a pleasant 30-minute walk from the fortress—described below (€2.80 one-way,

€4.10 round-trip, normally Tue-Sun 8:00-21:00, Mon until 19:00, July-Aug daily until 23:00). The **funicular** starts from Festungsgasse and ascends inside the fortress complex.

▲▲Hohensalzburg Fortress (Festung)

Built on a rock 400 feet above the Salzach River, this mighty castle has overlooked the Old Town for a thousand years. Today, it offers incredible views, pleasant cafés, and a handful of mediocre museums about medieval history.

The fortress is an eight-acre complex of some 50 buildings, courtyards, and protective walls. The **InfoPoint and Panorama Exhibition (A)** features a light introduction to the history of Salzburg and a tower climb with a commanding view. As you exit, pause at the "Salzburger Bull," a mechanical barrel organ used to wake the citizens every morning. The **Fortress Museum (Festungsmuseum, B)** exhibit shows how the fortress was constructed, along with a great town model and military artifacts. The **State Rooms (Fürstenzimmer, C)** are the most beautiful in the palace, with richly painted and gilded woodwork.

The Marionette Exhibit has puppets and scenery backdrops of this Salzburg tradition (think of the "Lonely Goatherd" scene in *The Sound of Music*).

▶ *Basic ticket*—*€13.30 by funicular, €10.30 by foot;* ***all-inclusive ticket** that includes state rooms—€16.60 by funicular, €12.60 by foot;* ***panorama ticket**—€11 by funicular, €8.50 by foot, only available May-Sept 8:30-10:00 & 18:00-20:00; museums open daily 8:30-20:00, Oct-April 9:30-17:00, +43 662 8424 3011, www.salzburg-burgen.at. Avoid waits for the funicular ascent with the Salzburg Card (which lets*

A pleasant courtyard at Hohensalzburg Fort

Mozart's presence permeates his hometown.

you skip to the head of the line) or by walking up. Or buy your ticket online before you visit.

▲Mönchsberg Walk

The paved, wooded walking path along the narrow ridgeline between the Mönchsberg elevator and the fortress is less than a mile long, well signed, and makes for a great quiet and shady 30-minute hike. The views of Salzburg are the main draw, but there's also a modern art museum, castle-like homes to ogle, and a couple of places for a scenic drink. You can start from either end: at the Fortress or at the Mönchsberg elevator.

In the New Town, North of the River

▲Mirabell Gardens and Palace (Mirabellgarten und Schloss)

These bubbly gardens, laid out in 1730 for the prince-archbishop, have been open to the public since 1850 (thanks to Emperor Franz Josef, who was rattled by the popular revolutions of 1848). The palace is worth a peek inside to see the Marble Hall (the prince-archbishop's former ballroom, now a popular wedding venue) and the ornate Angel's Staircase.

▶ *The gardens and palace are free to enter. Gardens—open until dusk; palace—open daily 8:00-18:00 and nightly during concerts.*

▲Mozart's Residence (Wohnhaus)

In the fall of 1773, when Wolfgang was 17—and his family was flush with money from years of touring—the Mozarts moved here from their cramped apartment on Getreidegasse. Aimed toward the Mozart connoisseur, the exhibits feature original Mozart family instruments and a good introductory video, as well as an informative audioguide. Other exhibits highlight Wolfgang's father Leopold (a loving nurturer of young Mozart or an exploiting Svengali?) and Mozart's sister Nannerl (Wolfgang's fellow child prodigy who grew up to lead a stable life as wife and mother). By the time Mozart was 25, he'd grown tired of his father, this house, and Salzburg, and he went on to Vienna—to more triumphs, but ultimately, a sad end.

▶ *€12, €18.50 combo-ticket with Mozart's Birthplace, daily July-Aug 8:30-19:00, Sept-June 9:00-17:30, Makartplatz 8, +43 662 8742 2740, www.mozarteum.at.*

Beyond the Center

▲▲Hellbrunn Palace and Gardens

The prince-archbishops' summer palace—four miles outside the city—is a nice getaway. Upon arrival, buy your ticket and get an entry time for the fountains (generally on the half-hour—if there's a wait until your fountain visit starts, you can see the palace first). The 45-minute palace audioguide takes you through a series of amazing 17th-century gardens where you get soaked by trick fountains. Then you're free to wander the delightful garden, see the *Sound of Music* gazebo, and tour the modest palace.

▶ *Grounds—free, open daily 6:30-21:00; palace—€13.50 ticket includes fountains and palace audioguide, daily 9:00-17:30, July-Aug until 18:00, April and Oct until 16:30, these are last-tour times, closed Nov-March; +43 662 820 3720, www.hellbrunn.at.*

Getting There: Take **bus** #25 from the train station or from the Rathaus stop by the Staatsbrücke bridge, and get off at the Schloss Hellbrunn stop (3-4/hour, 20 minutes from station). In good weather, it's a delightful 30-minute **bike** excursion (see "Bike Rides" under "Activities in Salzburg," later).

Sights Outside Salzburg

If you have more time, you can day-trip to the nearby **Hallein Salt Mine** (www.salzwelten.at) or **Berchtesgaden** (alpine scenery and Hitler's Eagle's Nest retreat, www.kehlsteinhaus.de).

Trick fountain at Hellbrunn Palace

Salzburg by bike—with a group or alone

ACTIVITIES IN SALZBURG

▲▲*The Sound of Music* Tours

Salzburg is the joyful setting of *The Sound of Music*. The Broadway musical and 1965 movie tell the story of a stern captain who hires a governess for his unruly children and ends up marrying her. Though the movie took plenty of Hollywood liberties, it's based on the actual Von Trapp family from Austria. They really did come from Salzburg. Maria really was a governess who became the captain's wife. They did sing in the Festival Hall, they did escape from the Nazis, and they ended up after the war in Vermont, where Maria passed away in 1987.

Salzburg has a number of *Sound of Music* sights—mostly locations where the movie was shot, but also some places associated with the real Von Trapps. Since they're scattered throughout greater Salzburg, taking a tour is the best way to see them efficiently. As a bonus, you'll get outside the city center into the lovely countryside.

By Minibus: Most of **Bob's Special Tours** are small groups and have a more laid-back camaraderie. Online bookings close three days prior to the tour date—after that, email, call, or stop by the office to reserve (€55 for adults; RS%—student price with this book if you pay cash and book directly, €50 for ages 7-21 and students with ID, €45 for kids 6 and under—includes required car seat but must reserve in advance; daily at 9:00 and 14:00 year-round, Rudolfskai 38, +43 662 849 511, www.bobstours.com, office@bobstours.com).

By Big Bus: Panorama Tours uses larger buses that depart from their smart kiosk at Mirabellplatz daily at 9:15 and 14:00 year-round (€50, RS%—€5 discount for *S.O.M.* tours if you pay in cash and book by phone or in person, book by calling +43 662 874 029 or +43 662 883 2110, www.panoramatours.com).

By Bike: Fräulein Maria's Bicycle Tour offers some exercise on an eight-mile pedal—and much better access to the in-town sights, which are skipped or viewed from afar on the bus tours. Meet your guide at the Mirabell Gardens (at Mirabellplatz 4, 50 yards to the left of palace entry). The tour is very family-friendly (€40 includes bike, €25 for ages 13-18, €20 for kids under 13, RS%—€2 discount with this book; daily April-Oct at 9:30, June-Aug also at 16:30, allow 3.5 hours, reservations required, +43 650 342 6297, www.mariasbicycletours.com).

Sound of Music Locations in Salzburg

Mirabell Gardens: Where the kids sing "Do-Re-Mi" around the Pegasus statue

Festival Hall: Where the real-life Von Trapps performed, and where (in the movie) they sing "Edelweiss"

St. Peter's Cemetery: Inspiration for the scene in which the family hides from Nazi guards (it was actually filmed on a Hollywood set)

Nonnberg Abbey: Where the nuns sing "How do you solve a problem like Maria?"

Leopoldskron Palace: The Von Trapps' idyllic lakeside home in the movie (though it wasn't their actual home)

Hellbrunn Palace Gardens: Current home of the gazebo in "Sixteen Going on Seventeen"

Bike Rides

Salzburg is great fun for cyclists. A simple ride along the Salzach River—with flat bike lanes on either side—is scenic and easy.

Or take a four-mile path to Hellbrunn Palace. Head east along the river on Rudolfskai. After passing the last bridge (Nonntaler Brücke), cut inland along Petersbrunnstrasse, until you reach the university and Akademiestrasse. Beyond it find the start of Freisaalweg, which becomes the delightful Hellbrunner Allee bike path...which leads directly to the palace.

A'Velo Radladen rents bikes on the Old Town side of the main bridge, Staatsbrücke (€14/4 hours, RS%—10 percent off with this book; daily 9:30-18:00, possibly later in summer, closed Nov-March and in bad weather, passport number for security deposit, +43 676 435 5950, www.avelo.at). Some hotels also loan bikes to guests.

Buggy Rides

The horse buggies (*Fiaker*) that congregate at Residenzplatz charge €52 for a 25-minute trot around the Old Town (www.salzburg.info, search for "Carriage Rides").

Boat Tours

City Cruise Line (a.k.a. Stadt Schiff-Fahrt) runs a 40-minute round-trip river cruise with recorded commentary (€16, 3-4/day April-Oct, no boats Nov-March). For a longer cruise, ride to Hellbrunn (€18 one-way, €38 includes palace admission and a ride back to the Old Town on a double-decker bus; April-Oct most days at 14:00, 40 minutes one-way). Boats leave from the Old Town side of the river just downstream of the Makartsteg bridge (+43 662 825 858, www.salzburghighlights. at).

MUSIC IN SALZBURG

Almost any night of the year, you'll find classical music concerts held in historic settings. Pick up the free events calendar brochure at the TI or check Salzburg.info (under "Events," click on "Classical Music"). Here are some of the perennial venues:

Classical Concerts: Concerts of Mozart's greatest hits are performed nearly nightly at **Hohensalzburg Fortress** (Festungskonzerte; €38-46, reserve at +43 662 825 858 or www.salzburghighlights.at). **Mirabell Palace** (Schlosskonzerte) offers more sophisticated programs and better musicians in a Baroque hall (€36-42, RS%—10 percent discount, use code "RICK10"; +43 662 904 700, www.salzburg-palace-concerts.com). With the **Mozart Dinner Concert,**

Enjoy classical music at classy venues.

Tasty chocolate "Mozart balls"

you get a candlelit meal in the historic St. Peter Stiftskulinarium restaurant (see "Sleeping and Eating in Salzburg," below) along with your Mozart music (€74-98, reserve by email or phone, +43 662 902 900, www.mozart-dinner-concert-salzburg.com, office@skg.co.at). The **Residenz** (Residenzkonzerte) hosts 45-minute Renaissance-era concerts most afternoons (€22, discount with Salzburg Card or DomQuartier ticket, +43 664 423 5645, www.agenturorpheus.at).

Marionette Theater: These operas with marionettes, a much-loved Salzburg tradition, enchant kids and adults (€25-40, Schwarzstrasse 24, +43 662 872 406, www.marionetten.at).

Sunday Morning Mass at Salzburg Cathedral: The 10:00 service generally features a Mass written by a well-known composer performed by a choir, organist, or other musicians. The worship service is often followed at 11:30 by a free organ concert (music program at www.kirchen.net/dommusik).

Salzburg Music Festival: The famous music festival from mid-July to the end of August brings large crowds. There are usually plenty of beds available, except for August weekends. Major musical events are expensive (€50-430) and sell out well in advance (bookable from January, www.salzburgerfestspiele.at).

SLEEPING AND EATING IN SALZBURG

Sleeping

These three places are in the New Town (north of the river), near a lively pedestrian street, a 10-minute walk from the Old Town: **$$$$ Altstadthotel Wolf-Dietrich** (Wolf-Dietrich-Strasse 7, +43 662 871 275, www.salzburg-hotel.at); **$$ Cityhotel Trumer Stube** (Bergstrasse 6, +43 662 874 776, www.trumer-stube.at); **$$ Gästehaus im Priesterseminar Salzburg** (Dreifaltigkeitsgasse 14, +43 662 8774 9510, www.gaestehaus-priesterseminar-salzburg.at).

These two hotels are centrally located in the Old Town, near Mozartplatz: **$$$$ Boutique Hotel am Dom** (Goldgasse 17, +43 662 842 765, www.hotelamdom.at); **$$$ Hotel Weisse Taube** (Kaigasse 9, www.weissetaube.at).

Outside of downtown, these great-value, rural pensions are an easy 15-minute ride on bus #21 from the Old Town: **$$ Hotel Pension Bloberger Hof** (Hammerauer Strasse 4, +43 662 830 227, www.

Salzburg—the Old Town and Hohensalzburg Fortress (on the hill), bordered by the Salzach River

blobergerhof.at); **$$ Pension Ballwein** (Moosstrasse 69a, +43 664 222 5396, www.pension-ballwein.at).

Eating

The following places are conveniently located in the Old Town. In Austria, smoking is still allowed in restaurants and bars; some restaurants have nonsmoking sections, but expect secondhand smoke wherever you sit. Fortunately for nonsmokers, many eateries offer plenty of outdoor seating.

$$ Gasthaus Wilder Mann offers traditional dishes geared to cold weather. While they have a few outdoor tables, the atmosphere is all indoors (Mon-Sat 11:00-21:00, closed Sun, Getreidegasse 20 to Griesgasse 17, +43 662 841 787, www.wildermann.co.at).

$$ St. Paul Stubm Beer Garden has a lederhosen-clad waitstaff and a decidedly untouristy atmosphere—better than at beer halls. Reservations are smart (Tue-Sat 17:00-22:00, closed Sun-Mon, Herrengasse 16, +43 662 843 220, www.paul-stube.at).

$$ Café Tomaselli serves a couple of light meals and lots of drinks and cakes. The café has fine seating on Alter Markt square and a view terrace upstairs (daily 7:00-19:00, Alter Markt 9, +43 662 844 488).

$$$$ Blaue Gans (The Blue Goose) has the most romantic ambience in the old center, with three dining areas and a traditional Austrian menu sprinkled with a splash of the Adriatic—Italy meets the Alps (Mon-Sat 12:00-22:00, closed Sun, Getreidegasse 41, +43 662 8424 9154).

$$$ Restaurant Triangel has a cozy, candlelit atmosphere, and a great traditional menu (daily 11:30-22:00, closed Sun-Mon in off-season, Wiener-Philharmonker-Gasse 7, +43 662 842 229).

$$$$ St. Peter Stiftskulinarium, reputedly in business for more than 1,000 years, offers a confusing mix of menus. Stick with the casual menu (Austrian/Mediterranean, €20-30 plates). Try to sit in the "outdoor" section, carved into the mountain (daily 12:00-22:00, at foot of Mönchsberg, +43 662 841 268).

Steingasse Pub Crawl: For a fun post-concert activity, drop in on a couple of atmospheric bars at the Linzer Gasse end of Steingasse. A few dark bars, each inviting yet with a different vibe, are within about 100 yards of each other (all open until the wee hours).

Practicalities

HELPFUL HINTS

Travel Tips

Travel Advisories: Before traveling, check updated health and safety conditions, including restrictions for your destination, at Travel. State.gov (US State Department travel pages) and CDC.gov (Centers for Disease Control and Prevention).

Tourist Information: Munich's helpful city-run TI is on the main square, Marienplatz, below the glockenspiel (Mon-Fri 10:00-18:00, Sat 9:00-17:00, Sun 10:00-14:00, +49 89 2339 6500, www.muenchen.de). A second TI is located outside the main train station at Luisenstrasse 1 (Tue-Sat 9:00-17:00, closed Sun).

Time Zones: Germany is six/nine hours ahead of the East/West Coasts of the US. For a handy time converter, use the world clock app on your phone or download one (see www.timeanddate.com).

Business Hours: Most shops are open from about 9:00 until 18:00-20:00 on weekdays; smaller stores generally close earlier on Saturdays, and nearly all stores are shut up tight on Sundays and public holidays, so you'll have to do your shopping the day before. Many museums and sights are closed on Monday. Catholic regions, including Bavaria, shut down during religious holidays.

Watt's Up? Europe's electrical system is 220 volts, instead of North America's 110 volts. Most electronics (laptops, phones, cameras) and appliances (newer hair dryers, CPAP machines) convert automatically, so you won't need a converter, but you will need an adapter plug with two round prongs, sold inexpensively at travel stores in the US.

Safety and Emergencies

Emergency and Medical Help: For any emergency service—ambulance, police, or fire—call **112** from a mobile phone or landline. If you get sick, do as the locals do and go to a pharmacist for advice. Or ask at your hotel for help—they'll know the nearest medical and emergency services.

Theft or Loss: To replace a **passport,** you'll need to go in person to an embassy in Berlin (passport replacement by appointment only Wed-Thu, sign up online, Clayallee 170, +49 30 83050, http://de.usembassy.gov). If your credit and debit cards disappear, cancel and replace them, and report the loss immediately (with a mobile phone, call these 24-hour US numbers: Visa—+1 303 967 1096, Mastercard—+1 636 722 7111, and American Express—+1 336 393 1111). For more information, see RickSteves.com/help.

Bikes and Pedestrians: The strip of pathway closest to the street is usually reserved for bikes. Pedestrians wandering into the bike path may hear the cheery ding-ding of a cyclist's bell just before being knocked unconscious. Look for blue-and-white street signs showing which lanes are for pedestrians and cyclists (or, sometimes, shared between them). The city's vision for the old center is one with no cars—just service vehicles, scooters, bikes, and pedestrians.

Around Town

Bookstore: The three-story Hugendubel bookstore on Karlsplatz has some English offerings (Mon-Sat 10:00-20:00, closed Sun, Karlsplatz 12, +49 89 3075 7575, www.hugendubel.de).

WCs: By law, any place serving beer must admit the public (whether or not they're customers) to use the WCs. Be bold and find relief.

Laundry: A half-block from the train station, **City Dry Clean** is a big, staffed self-service launderette (long hours daily, drop-off service available from about 7:00, Bayerstrasse 6, +49 160 825 4178).

ARRIVAL IN MUNICH

Munich Airport

Munich Airport (Flughafen München) is 17 miles northeast of town (code: MUC, www.munich-airport.de). It has two large terminals: Lufthansa and its partners (including United) use Terminal 2, while the older Terminal 1 serves most other airlines. A shuttle bus lets connecting passengers transfer between terminals without exiting security. Outside security, it's a 10-minute walk.

In between the two terminals is a shopping and services complex with a supermarket, eateries, ATMs, car rental, and—underneath—the airport's handy S-Bahn station.

To get between Munich Airport and downtown, you have these options:

Subway: It's an easy 50-minute ride from Marienplatz or the main train station on the S-1 or S-8 **suburban train** (both run every

Helpful Websites

Munich Tourist Information: Muenchen.de
German Tourist Information: Germany.travel
Passports and Red Tape: Travel.State.gov
Cheap Flights: Flights.Google.com (international flights), SkyScanner.com (flights within Europe)
Airplane Carry-on Restrictions: TSA.gov
European Train Schedules: Bahn.com
General Travel Tips: RickSteves.com (train travel, rail passes, car rental, travel insurance, packing lists, and more

20 minutes, from 4:00 to after midnight). From either terminal, ride the escalator down to the train platforms, buy a ticket from the machines (choose the "with validation" option to save having to stamp it), and look at the monitors to see which train will get you into the city most quickly.

Returning from the city to the airport, the S-8 is easier, as the S-1 line has two branches and trains split at Neufahrn. If you ride the S-1 to the airport, be certain you're in the part of the train that's going to the Flughafen (airport)—signs and announcements help.

The airport is in public transport zone 5; an M-5 ticket costs €12.30 for one person and includes any transfers en route. But the M-5 all-day pass (€13.70) is worth getting if you'll be making even one more public transport trip that day. Groups of two or more can buy the €25.70 all-day partner ticket (Partner-Tageskarte), which covers up to five adults for the day.

Lufthansa Airport Bus: This bus links the airport with the main train station (€11, €17.50 round-trip, 3/hour, 45 minutes, buses depart airport 6:30-22:30, depart train station 5:15-19:55, buy tickets on bus or online in advance; from inside the station, exit near track 26 and look for yellow Airport Bus signs; www.airportbus-muenchen.de).

Taxi: Avoid taking a taxi from the airport—it's a long, expensive drive. Take public transit to the city and then switch to a taxi if needed.

Munich's Train Station (Hauptbahnhof)

Munich's main train station (München Hauptbahnhof) is in the midst of a massive, multiyear renovation: Services mentioned here may be suspended or relocate as construction progresses.

Suburban trains, subway lines, trams, and buses connect the station to the rest of the city (though many of my recommended hotels are within walking distance). For the S-Bahn or U-Bahn, take the escalators by track 26 down into the underground concourse, turn right, and follow the signs. Buses depart from the streets on both the north and south sides of the station. The station has tram stops on three sides—the useful #16, #17, and #18 trams all use the plain Hauptbahnhof stop at the east end.

Look for the *Reisezentrum* (travel center, with ticket counters) near track 11. Clean, high-tech, pay WCs are downstairs near tracks 11 and 26. You'll find lockers opposite track 26. Bike rental is by track 32.

GETTING AROUND MUNICH

Much of Munich is walkable, but for trips beyond the historic core, it's worth learning the public transit system and probably getting a day pass.

By Public Transit

Munich's transit system includes buses, trams, and two types of trains: U-Bahn (subway) and S-Bahn (suburban train). Transit lines are numbered (for example, S-3 or U-5), and there are seven concentric fare zones (Zone M and Zones 1-6). You'll spend most of your time in Zone M (central Munich). You might also travel to Zone 1 (Dachau) and Zone 5 (the airport)

Ticket Options: Transit tickets are sold at any ticket machine that has an MVG (blue machines) or DB (red machines) logo.

A **regular ticket** (*Einzelfahrkarte*) for Zone M costs €3.50 and is good for three hours in one direction, including changes and stops. For short rides (four stops max, only two of which can be on the subway), buy the €1.80 short-stretch ticket (*Kurzstrecke*), good for one ride.

Day tickets (*Single-Tageskarte*) for Zone M (€8.20) pay for themselves if you take three regular trips, and can be a great deal for a busy traveler. If you're going to Dachau, buy the M-1 version of the *Single-Tageskarte* (€9.30, covers Zones M and 1). For the airport (*Flughafen*), you need an M-5 ticket for zones M through 5 (€12.30/single ride; €13.70/all-day pass).

All-day small-group passes (*Partner-Tageskarte*) cover all public transportation for up to five adults (or up to two adults and six kids). A *Partner-Tageskarte* for Zone M costs €15.60. An M-1 group ticket (covering Zones M and 1, which includes Dachau) costs €17, and an M-5 group ticket valid out to the airport (*Flughafen*) costs €25.70. Even two people traveling together save money, and for groups, it's a steal. The only catch is that you've got to stay together.

Using the System: Tickets must be validated prior to using them. (For an all-day or multiday pass, stamp it only the first time you use it.) Some machines issue prevalidated tickets, or ask you to choose whether to validate at the time of purchase—if you say "yes" to validation, you're all set.

If you have an unvalidated ticket, on the S-Bahn and U-Bahn, punch it in the blue machine before going down to the platform. For buses and trams, stamp your ticket once on board. Plainclothes ticket checkers enforce this honor system, rewarding freeloaders with €60 fines.

Useful Transit Lines: All S-Bahn lines (S-1 through S-8) run east-west along the same main axis between the Hauptbahnhof, Marienplatz, and the Ostbahnhof, peeling off to various destinations at either end. If you're traveling within this central zone, it doesn't matter which S-Bahn line number you take. One track (*Gleis*) will be headed east to the Ostbahnhof, the other west to the Hauptbahnhof. Hop on any train going your direction.

The U-3 goes to Olympic Park and the BMW sights.

Trams take you where the U-Bahn doesn't.

Covering the sights by bike, with a guide

The S-2 goes to Dachau.

Bus #100 runs from the train station past most of the art museums, as well as the English Garden.

Tram #17 goes to Nymphenburg Palace (from the train station and Sendlinger Tor).

Tram #16 whisks you from the train station around the south edge of the old center and up to the English Garden.

By Taxi or Private Driver

Taxis are honest and professional, and Uber works just like at home, but both are generally unnecessary (call +49 89 21610 for a taxi). Private driver **Johann Fayoumi** is reliable and speaks English, and can take up to eight passengers (€80/hour, +49 174 183 8473, www.firstclasslimousines.de, johannfayoumi@gmail.com).

By Bike

Level, compact, and with plenty of bike paths, Munich feels made for those on two wheels. When biking in Munich, follow these simple rules: Walk your bike through pedestrian zones; feel free to take your bike on the U- and S-Bahn, but not during rush hour (Mon-Fri 6:00-9:00 & 16:00-18:00) and only if you buy a €3.10 bike day pass (*Fahrrad-Tageskarte*); and follow the rules of the road, just like those driving cars.

Bike Rental Shops: These places provide helmets, maps, and route advice, and also offer bike tours. **Radius Tours** (*Rad* means "bike" in German) is in the train station in front of track 32 (€4/hour, €16/day, €30/2 days for basic bikes, RS%, daily 9:30-19:00, May-Aug until 20:00, closed Nov-March, +49 89 543 487 7730, www.radiustours.com). **Mike's Bike Tours** is in the old center (€10 for first hour, €2/additional hour, €18/day, RS%; daily 10:00-19:30, shorter hours off-season and closed in winter; Bräuhausstrasse 10—enter around corner on Hochbrückenstrasse; +49 89 2314 0263, www.mikesbiketours.com).

Tipping

Tipping in Germany isn't as automatic and generous as it is in the US. However, tips are appreciated and expected. Some general guidelines apply.

Restaurants: At restaurants that have a wait staff, tip by rounding up (about 10 percent) after a good meal. If paying with a credit card, be prepared to tip separately with cash or coins.

Taxis: For a typical ride, round up your fare a bit (for instance, if your fare is €4.70, pay €5).

Services: For local guides, private drivers, or others who spend several hours with you, and significantly improve the quality of your trip, a healthy tip (of around 10 percent) is not extravagant. In general, if someone in the tourism or service industry does a super job for you, a small tip of a euro or two is appropriate. If you're not sure whether (or how much) to tip, ask a local for advice.

MONEY

Germany uses the euro currency: 1 euro (€) = about $1.10. To convert prices in euros to dollars, add about 10 percent: €20 = about $22, €50 = about $55. Check Oanda.com for the latest exchange rates.

You'll use your **credit card** for purchases both big (hotels, advance tickets) and small (little shops, food stands). A "tap-to-pay" or "contactless" card is the most widely accepted and simplest to use. Check to see if you already have—or can get—a tap-to-pay version of your credit card (look on the card for the tap-to-pay symbol—four curvy lines). Make sure you know the numeric, four-digit PIN for each of your cards, both debit and credit. Request it if you don't have one, as it may be required for some purchases.

Use a **debit card** at ATMs (in Germany ask for a *Geldautomat*) to withdraw a small amount of local cash. While most transactions are by card these days, cash can help you out of a jam if your card randomly doesn't work, and can be useful to pay for things like tips and local guides. Keep your backup cards and cash safe in a **money belt.**

At self-service payment machines (such as transit-ticket kiosks), US cards may not work. In this case, look for a cashier who can process your card manually—or pay in cash.

STAYING CONNECTED

Making International Calls

From a Mobile Phone: Phone numbers in this book are presented exactly as you would dial them from a US mobile phone. For international access, press and hold 0 (zero) to get a + sign, then dial the country code (49 for Germany, 43 for Austria) and phone number.

From a US Landline to Europe: Replace + with 011 (US/Canada access code), then dial the country code (49 for Germany, 43 for Austria) and phone number.

From a European Landline to the US or Europe: Replace + with 00 (Europe access code), then dial the country code (49 for Germany, 43 for Austria, 1 for the US) and phone number. For more phoning help, see HowToCallAbroad.com.

Using Your Phone in Europe

Sign up for an international plan. To stay connected at a lower cost, sign up for an international service plan through your carrier. Most providers offer a simple bundle that includes calling, messaging, and data.

Use free Wi-Fi whenever possible. Unless you have an unlimited-data plan, save most of your online tasks for Wi-Fi. Most accommodations

One key to Munich's livability is its combination of traditional culture and modern convenience.

in Europe offer free Wi-Fi, and many cafés offer hotspots for customers. You may also find Wi-Fi at TIs, city squares, major museums, public-transit hubs, airports, and aboard trains and buses.

Save large-data tasks for Wi-Fi. If your included data is slow or metered, wait until you're on Wi-Fi to Skype or FaceTime, download apps, stream videos, or do other megabyte-greedy tasks. Using a navigation app such as Google Maps over a cellular network can require lots of data, so download maps when you're on Wi-Fi, then use the app offline.

Use Wi-Fi calling and messaging apps. Skype, FaceTime, and Google Meet are great for making free or low-cost calls or sending texts over Wi-Fi worldwide. WhatsApp is especially popular with Europeans, and is often the easiest way to communicate with guides, drivers, or other local contacts.

RESOURCES FROM RICK STEVES

Begin your trip at RickSteves.com: This book is just one of many in my series on European travel. I also produce a public television series, *Rick Steves' Europe,* and a public radio show, *Travel with Rick Steves.* My mobile-friendly website is *the* place to explore Europe in preparation for your trip. You'll find thousands of fun articles, beautiful photos, videos, and radio interviews; a wealth of money-saving tips; travel news dispatches; a video library of travel talks; our latest guidebook updates (RickSteves.com/update); and the free Rick Steves Audio Europe app with audio tours of Europe's top sights. You can also follow me on Facebook, Instagram, and Twitter.

Packing Checklist

Clothing

- ❑ 5 shirts: long- & short-sleeve
- ❑ 2 pairs pants (or skirts/capris)
- ❑ 1 pair shorts
- ❑ 5 pairs underwear & socks
- ❑ 1 pair walking shoes
- ❑ Sweater or warm layer
- ❑ Rainproof jacket with hood
- ❑ Tie, scarf, belt, and/or hat
- ❑ Swimsuit
- ❑ Sleepwear/loungewear

Money

- ❑ Debit card(s)
- ❑ Credit card(s)
- ❑ Hard cash (US $100-200)
- ❑ Money belt

Documents

- ❑ Passport
- ❑ Other required ID: Vaccine card/Covid test, entry visa, etc.
- ❑ Driver's license, student ID, hostel card, etc.
- ❑ Tickets & confirmations: flights, hotels, trains, rail pass, car rental, sight entries
- ❑ Photocopies of important documents
- ❑ Insurance details
- ❑ Guidebooks & maps
- ❑ Extra passport photos
- ❑ Notepad & pen
- ❑ Journal

Toiletries

- ❑ Soap, shampoo, toothbrush, toothpaste, floss, deodorant, sunscreen, brush/comb, etc.
- ❑ Medicines & vitamins
- ❑ First-aid kit
- ❑ Glasses/contacts/sunglasses
- ❑ Face masks & hand sanitizer
- ❑ Sewing kit
- ❑ Packet of tissues (for WC)
- ❑ Earplugs

Electronics

- ❑ Mobile phone
- ❑ Camera & related gear
- ❑ Tablet/ebook reader/laptop
- ❑ Headphones/earbuds
- ❑ Chargers & batteries
- ❑ Plug adapters

Miscellaneous

- ❑ Daypack
- ❑ Sealable plastic baggies
- ❑ Laundry supplies
- ❑ Small umbrella
- ❑ Travel alarm/watch

Optional Extras

- ❑ Second pair of shoes
- ❑ Travel hairdryer
- ❑ Disinfecting wipes
- ❑ Water bottle
- ❑ Fold-up tote bag
- ❑ Small flashlight & binoculars
- ❑ Small towel or washcloth
- ❑ Tiny lock

German Survival Phrases

In the phonetics, ī sounds like the long i in "light," and bolded syllables are stressed.

Hello.	Hallo.	**hah**-loh
Good day.	Guten Tag.	**goo**-tehn tahg
Do you speak English?	Sprechen Sie Englisch? **shprehkh**-ehn zee **ehng**-lish	
Yes. / No.	Ja. / Nein.	yah / nīn
I (don't) understand.	Ich verstehe (nicht).	ikh fehr-**shtay**-heh (nikht)
Please.	Bitte.	**bit**-teh
Thank you.	Danke.	**dahng**-keh
I'm sorry.	Es tut mir leid.	ehs toot meer līt
Excuse me.	Entschuldigung.	ehnt-**shool**-dig-oong
Goodbye.	Auf Wiedersehen.	owf **vee**-der-zayn
one / two / three	eins / zwei / drei	īns / tsvī / drī
How much is it?	Wieviel kostet das?	**vee**-feel **kohs**-teht dahs
I'd like / We'd like...	Ich hätte gern / Wir hätten gern... ikh **heh**-teh gehrn / veer **heh**-tehn gehrn	
...a room.	...ein Zimmer.	īn **tsim**-mer
...a ticket to ____.	...eine Fahrkarte nach ____. ī-neh **far**-kar-teh nahkh	
Where is...?	Wo ist...?	voh ist
...the train station	...der Bahnhof	dehr **bahn**-hohf
...tourist information	...das Touristen-informations-büro dahs too-**ris**-tehn-in-for-maht-see-**ohns**-bew-roh	
...the toilet	...die Toilette	dee toh-**leh**-teh
men / women	Herren / Damen	**hehr**-rehn / **dah**-mehn
left / right	links / rechts	links / **rehkhts**
straight	geradeaus	geh-**rah**-deh-**ows**
What time does this open / close?	Um wieviel Uhr wird hier geöffnet / geschlossen? oom **vee**-feel oor veerd heer geh-**urf**-neht / geh-**shloh**-sehn	
now / soon / later	jetzt / bald / später	yehtst / bahld / **shpay**-ter
today / tomorrow	heute / morgen	**hoy**-teh / **mor**-gehn

In a German Restaurant

I'd like / We'd like...	Ich hätte gern / Wir hätten gern... ikh **heh**-teh gehrn / veer **heh**-tehn gehrn
...a reservation for...	...eine Reservierung für... ī-neh reh-zer-**feer**-oong fewr
...a table for one / two.	...einen Tisch für eine Person / zwei Personen. ī-nehn tish fewr ī-neh pehr-**zohn** / tsvī pehr-**zoh**-nehn
...the menu (in English).	...die Speisekarte (auf Englisch), bitte. dee **shpī**-zeh-kar-teh (owf **ehng**-lish) **bit**-teh
service (not) included	Trinkgeld (nicht) inklusive **trink**-gehlt (nikht) in-kloo-**zee**-veh
to go	zum Mitnehmen tsoom **mit**-nay-mehn
with / without	mit / ohne mit / **oh**-neh
and / or	und / oder oont / **oh**-der
menu (of the day)	(Tages-) Karte (**tah**-gehs-) **kar**-teh
specialty of the house	Spezialität des Hauses **shpayt**-see-ah-lee-**tayt** dehs **how**-zehs
appetizers	Vorspeise **for**-shpī-zeh
bread / cheese	Brot / Käse broht / **kay**-zeh
sandwich	Sandwich **zahnd**-vich
soup / salad	Suppe / Salat **zup**-peh / zah-**laht**
meat / poultry	Fleisch / Geflügel flīsh / geh-**flew**-gehl
fish / seafood	Fisch / Meeresfrüchte fish / **mee**-rehs-**froysh**-teh
fruit / vegetables	Obst / Gemüse ohpst / geh-**mew**-zeh
dessert	Nachspeise **nahkh**-shpī-zeh
coffee / tea	Kaffee / Tee kah-**fay** / tay
wine / beer	Wein / Bier vīn / beer
red / white	rot / weiss roht / vīs
glass / bottle	Glas / Flasche glahs / **flah**-sheh
Cheers!	Prost! prohst
The bill, please.	Rechnung, bitte. **rehkh**-noong **bit**-teh
tip	Trinkgeld **trink**-gehlt
Delicious!	Lecker! **lehk**-er

For more user-friendly German phrases, check out *Rick Steves German Phrase Book.*

INDEX

Start your trip at

Our website enhances this book and turns

Explore Europe

At ricksteves.com you can browse through thousands of articles, videos, photos and radio interviews, plus find a wealth of money-saving travel tips for planning your dream trip. And with our mobile-friendly website, you can easily access all this great travel information anywhere you go.

TV Shows

Preview the places you'll visit by watching entire half-hour episodes of *Rick Steves' Europe* (choose from all 100 shows) on-demand, for free.

ricksteves.com

your travel dreams into affordable reality

Radio Interviews

Enjoy ready access to Rick's vast library of radio interviews covering travel tips and cultural insights that relate specifically to your Europe travel plans.

Travel Forums

Learn, ask, share! Our online community of savvy travelers is a great resource for first-time travelers to Europe, as well as seasoned pros.

Travel News

Subscribe to our free Travel News e-newsletter, and get monthly updates from Rick on what's happening in Europe.

Classroom Europe®

Check out our free resource for educators with 500 short video clips from the *Rick Steves' Europe* TV show.

Audio Europe™

Rick's Free Travel App

Get your FREE Rick Steves Audio Europe™ app to enjoy...

- Dozens of self-guided tours of Europe's top museums, sights and historic walks
- Hundreds of tracks filled with cultural insights and sightseeing tips from Rick's radio interviews
- All organized into handy geographic playlists
- For Apple and Android

With Rick whispering in your ear, Europe gets even better.

Find out more at ricksteves.com

Pack Light and Right

Gear up for your next adventure at ricksteves.com

Light Luggage

Pack light and right with Rick Steves' affordable, custom-designed rolling carry-on bags, backpacks, day packs and shoulder bags.

Accessories

From packing cubes to moneybelts and beyond, Rick has personally selected the travel goodies that will help your trip go smoother.

Shop at ricksteves.com

Rick Steves has

Experience maximum Europe

Save time and energy

This guidebook is your independent-travel toolkit. But for all it delivers, it's still up to you to devote the time and energy it takes to manage the preparation and logistics that are essential for a happy trip. If that's a hassle, there's a solution.

Rick Steves Tours

A Rick Steves tour takes you to Europe's most interesting places with great guides and small groups.